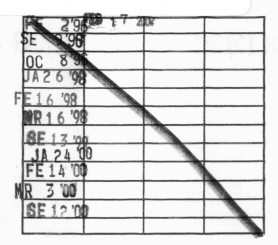

THE
FIRST
FREEDOM

RELIGION & THE BILL OF RIGHTS

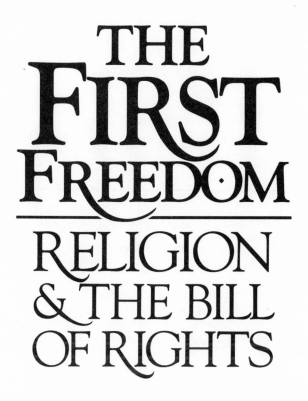

JAMES E. WOOD, JR.
EDITOR

J.M. DAWSON INSTITUTE OF CHURCH-STATE STUDIES
Baylor University • Waco, Texas 76798-7308

Published by the J.M. Dawson Institute of Church-State Studies at
Baylor University on
Lake Brazos at
Waco, Texas 78798-7308
USA

THE FIRST FREEDOM:
RELIGION AND THE BILL OF RIGHTS

Address correspondence to
J.M. Dawson Institute of Church-State Studies
B.U. Box 7308, Baylor University, Waco, Texas 76798 USA

FIRST EDITION 1990

Library of Congress Cataloging-in-Publication Data
Preassigned Catalog Card Number: 90-060921

International Standard Book Numbers:
ISBN 0-929182-13-8 (CLOTH)   ISBN 0-929182-14-6 (PAPER)

Prepared camera ready by the publications staff of J.M. Dawson Institute of
Church-State Studies using MASS-11 ™ Version 8.0 © Microsystems Engineer-
ing Corporation on VAX 8700 minicomputer by Digital Equipment Corporation
printing to Varityper VT600W using Palatino typeface. The latter is trademarked
by Allied Corporation. Software licensed to Baylor University.

Contents

PREFACE

All the essays in this volume were expressly prepared for a symposium held at Baylor University, 17-18 April 1989, convened and sponsored by the J. M. Dawson Institute of Church-State Studies, to commemorate the bicentennial of the adoption of the American Bill of Rights by the Congress in 1789. Ratification, of course, did not come until a little over two years later in 1791. While all of the essays were prepared first for presentation at the symposium, they were also specifically written for publication in this volume and, therefore, as original essays have not been published elsewhere.

The American Bill of Rights, which includes the first ten amendments of the Constitution, played a decisive role in the history of the Constitution. First, the promise of the adoption of a bill of rights helped ensure the ultimate ratification of the Constitution by the states and, second, the adoption of the Bill of Rights helped to ensure the longevity of the Constitution by convincingly demonstrating the applicability of the amending process.

These essays are published as a fitting tribute to the bicentennial of the Bill of Rights. Four of the authors write from their grounding in American religious history, while three of the authors write from the perspective of their expertise in American constitutional law. Particular attention is given in this volume to the historical context of the adoption of the First Amendment and the original intent of the framers of the religion clauses in the light of the applications and judicial interpretations given them today.

As would be expected, the symposium provoked lively discussions following each of the papers presented. The last session of the symposium was devoted to dialogue and discussion with a panel of all the presenters which included extended exchanges between the presenters as well as with the symposium participants, more than two hundred of whom had registered from numerous colleges and universities and were representative of a variety of academic disciplines. The essays reflect the insights and interpretations of scholars and specialists on American church-state relations. These essays are being published at a time when there is growing clamor for a reexamination of the religion clauses of the First Amendment, the "First Freedom" of the Bill of Rights, both as to the clauses' original intent and their appropriate application in contemporary American society.

Special acknowledgment is made here to the authors of the papers presented at the symposium and the special preparation given by the authors to the writing of these essays for publication in this volume. Without their manifestly scholarly competence and incisive analyses of their subjects, the quality of their presentations at the symposium and the publication of their essays in this volume would have been greatly diminished. To all the symposium participants, we are grateful. In addition, grateful appreciation is here expressed to Robert M. Baird, Charles W. Barrow, Rosalie Beck, James A. Curry, David M. Guinn, David W. Hendon, Glenn O. Hilburn, David L. Long-fellow, Robert T. Miller, Harold W. Osborne, Bob E. Patterson, Robert L. Reid, Rufus B. Spain, and Stuart E. Rosenbaum for assisting in the planning and convening of the symposium, and to Wanda Gilbert for her assistance in coordinating mailings and program plans for the symposium. We are grateful to Herbert H. Reynolds, President of Baylor University, for his strong encouragement and support and for the special participation of John S. Belew, Provost and Executive Vice President of Academic Affairs of Baylor University. My special gratitude is here expressed to Marion Travis for her editorial assistance and for being responsible for creating the camera ready copy for the desktop publishing of this volume, in which she was ably assisted by Perry Glanzer and Lana Magers. I am pleased also to acknowledge Brett Latimer for his assistance with the index.

It is hoped that these essays will appeal to a wide range of readers, specialists and non-specialists alike, and that this volume will contribute to enlightened debate and renewed appreciation of the meaning and significance of the "First Freedom" of the Bill of Rights.

James E. Wood, Jr.

Baylor University
Spring 1990

CONTRIBUTORS

HENRY C. ABRAHAM is James Hart Professor of Government and Foreign Affairs, University of Virginia. His publications include *Freedom and the Court: Civil Rights and Liberties in the United States; The Judicial Process: An Introductory Analysis of the Courts of the United States, England, and France; The Judiciary: The Supreme Court in the Governmental Process; Justices and Presidents: A Political History of Appointments to the Supreme Court* and numerous articles in a wide variety of scholarly journals.

EDWIN S. GAUSTAD is Professor of History, University of California, Riverside. His works include *The Great Awakening; Historical Atlas of Religion in America; Dissent in American Religion; Documentary History of Religion in America; Faith of Our Fathers: Religion and the New Nation*, coeditor of a six-volume series on *The Bible in American Culture*, the recently published revised edition of *A Religious History of America*, and numerous articles in books and a variety of scholarly journals.

DOUGLAS LAYCOCK is Alice McKean Young Regents Chair in Law, University of Texas. His publications include *Modern American Remedies: Cases and Materials* and *The Death of the Irreparable Injury Rule* (forthcoming). He has published articles in *The Texas Law Review, Columbia Law Review, Harvard Law Review*, and the *Yale Law Journal*.

DAVID LITTLE is Senior Scholar at the U. S. Institute of Peace in Washington, D. C. His publications include *Religion, Order, and Law: A Study in Prerevolutionary England; Comparative Religious Ethics: A New Method* (coauthor); *American Foreign Policy and Moral Rhetoric: The Example of Vietnam; Human Rights and the Conflicts of Culture: Freedom of Religion and Conscience in the West and Islam* (coauthor), *Rights and Emergencies: Protecting Human Rights in the Midst of Conflict* and numerous articles in various scholarly journals.

LEO PFEFFER is Adjunct Professor of Political Science, Long Island University, New York. His publications include *The Liberties of an American; Creeds in Competition; Church, State, and Freedom; Church and State in the United States* (coauthor); *This Honorable Court; God, Caesar, and the Constitution; Religious Freedom;* and *Religion, State, and the Burger Court.* His articles on church and state have appeared in a wide range of scholarly journals, books, and encyclopedias.

JOHN F. WILSON is Agate Brown and George L. Collord Professor of Religion and Director of the Project on Church and State in American Culture, Princeton University. His publications include *Public Religion in American Culture; Pulpit and Parliament: Puritanism During the English Civil Wars, 1640-1648; Church and State in American History;* and *Church and State in America: A Bibliographical Guide* (2 vols.). He has published numerous essays in a variety of books and scholarly journals.

JAMES E. WOOD, JR. is Ethel and Simon Bunn Professor of Church-State Studies and Director of the J. M. Dawson Institute of Church-State Studies, Baylor University. His publications include *Church and State in Scripture, History, and Constitutional Law* (coauthor); *Nationhood and the Kingdom; Religion and Politics; Religion, the State, and Education; Religion and the State: Essays in Honor of Leo Pfeffer;* and *Readings on Church and State.* Founding editor of *Journal of Church and State,* he is the author of numerous articles in a variety of books and scholarly journals.

INTRODUCTION

Religion and the Constitution

JAMES E. WOOD, JR.

More than two hundred years ago, fifty-five delegates from twelve of the thirteen original states (Rhode Island abstained from participating) met in Philadelphia, 25 May-17 September 1787, and drafted a document that would become the Constitution of the United States. In a real sense, the Constitutional Convention of 1787 represented the founding of this nation and the establishment of its republican form of government.

Among the delegates twenty-six were college graduates; three were by profession college professors; two were college presidents; four had read law at the Inns of Court in London; twenty-eight had served in Congress and most of the others had served in state legislatures; and nine were foreign born. Five of the delegates were under thirty years of age; Alexander Hamilton was thirty and James Madison was barely thirty-six. Only four of the delegates were beyond sixty years of age. Benjamin Franklin at eighty-one was the oldest delegate by at least fifteen years.

The result of their efforts was a document that has become the oldest national constitution in the world and has been widely heralded as "the most successful constitution in history."[1] As the last signatures were added to the document, Benjamin Franklin raised his eyes to look at a painting of a rising or setting sun behind the chair of the presiding officer, George Washington, and prophetically remarked: "I have often and often in the course of the Session, and the vicissitudes of my hopes and fears as to its issue, looked at that behind the President without being able to tell whether it was rising or setting: But now at length I have the happiness to know that it is a rising and not a setting Sun."[2]

Franklin's vision of the future importance of the document was not shared by many of the other delegates. Alexander Hamilton described the Constitution as a "weak and worthless fabric."[3] Just a few days before the Convention concluded its work, James Madison wrote despairingly to Thomas Jefferson that the Constitution about to be adopted "will neither effectually answer its national object nor prevent the local mischiefs which every where excite disgusts agst the state governments."[4] Fortunately, partly in response to expressed opposition to the Constitution, "Within a few days," as Robert A. Rutland has noted, "Madison rapidly changed from a lukewarm supporter to become the boldest advocate for the proposed constitution."[5] Along with most of the delegates, however, Madison thought it would last but a generation. But, as Samuel Eliot Morrison observed one hundred seventy-five years later, "Ben Franklin's prophecy that, with all its faults, no better could be obtained, has proved to be correct."[6]

While delegates to the Constitutional Convention were well aware of the persecution of dissenters and nonconformists in colonial America and in England, scarce consideration was given to the subject of religion at the Convention during those summer months of 1787. Both prominent political leaders in the colonies as well as members of the clergy had argued that religion "is a concern between God and the soul, with which no human authority can intermeddle."[7] Nevertheless, a major step was taken with respect to religion that is all too often overlooked. When reviewing the constitutional provisions with respect to religion there is a tendency to focus almost exclusively on the religion clauses of the Bill of Rights, while overlooking the historical and substantive significance of Clause 3 of Article VI: "No religious Test shall ever be required as a qualification to any Office or public trust under the United States."[8] Introduced by Charles C. Pinckney, a South Carolina delegate, the proposal passed unanimously and "without much debate," as reported later by Luther Martin, a Maryland delegate to the Convention.[9] While this provision would later provoke vigorous debate in the ratifying state conventions, as Edwin S. Gaustad notes in his essay (pp. 41-59), the adoption of this provision virtually precluded the establishment of a state church. Supreme Court Justice Joseph Story (1812-1845) wrote in his *Commentaries on the Constitution of the United States*, "This clause is not introduced merely for the purpose of satisfying the scruples of many respectable persons, who feel an invincible repugnance to any religious test, or affirmation. It had a higher object; to cut off for ever every pretence of any alliance between church and state in the national government."[10]

One curious form of discrimination, however, emerged after independence. Aided by a wave of anticlericalism from prerevolutionary France, steps were taken by the states to bar members of the clergy from holding public office, particularly as members of state legislatures. By the time of the adoption of the Constitution, with its exclusion of any religious test for office, a majority of the original states had constitutional provisions prohibiting members of the clergy from serving in state legislatures (Maryland, Virginia, North Carolina, and Georgia) and, in some cases, from holding any political or public office (New York, Delaware, and South Carolina). With the ratification of the federal Constitution, including Article VI of "no religious test" for public office, discrimination against the clergy's holding federal office was expressly prohibited.

During the nineteenth century, the disabilities against the clergy were gradually removed by the states, except Maryland and Tennessee, which continued to bar members of the clergy from serving in their legislatures until the 1970s. Finally, in a case out of Tennessee, the last of the state laws barring clergy from state office was unanimously declared unconstitutional by the United States Supreme Court in *McDaniel v. Paty* (1978).[11]

Three months after the Constitutional Convention had adjourned in Philadelphia, Oliver Ellsworth, a delegate to the Convention from Connecticut and later chief justice of the United States Supreme Court (1796-1800), in response to critics of Article VI, Section 3, cogently argued that the Constitutional provision denying any religious test for federal office was not unfavorable to religion but simply served to prohibit religious discrimination and to affirm the right of religious freedom. In doing so, he wrote, the new national government was but fulfilling its rightful role to serve its citizens.

The business of a civil government is to protect the citizen in his rights, to defend the community from hostile power, and to promote the general welfare. Civil government has no business to meddle with the private opinions of the people. If I demean myself as a good citizen, I am accountable, not to man, but to God, for the religious opinions which I embrace, and the manner in which I worship the supreme being. If such had been the universal sentiments of mankind, and they had acted accordingly, persecution, the bane of truth and of error, with her bloody axe and flaming hand, would never have turned so great a part of the world into a field of blood.[12]

In the debate in Massachusetts over ratification of the Constitution, when objection was raised over the Constitutional provision of no religious test for federal office, a prominent member of the clergy argued that it was appropriate because of the very nature of religion. "The great object of religion being God supreme, and the seat of religion in man being the heart of conscience, i.e., reason God has given us, employed on our moral actions, in their most important consequences, as related to the tribunal of God, hence I infer that God alone is the God of the conscience, and, consequently, attempts to erect human tribunals for the consciences of men are impious encroachments upon the prerogatives of God." Indeed, he concluded, "had there been a religious test as a qualification for office, it would . . . have been a great blemish" on the Constitution.[13]

It is not appropriate here to review the ratification of the Constitution, since this subject is addressed in the second essay of this volume. Suffice it to say, ratification of the Constitution by the required three-fourths of the states came within nine months, with all states ratifying the Constitution by May 1790,[14] but not without serious objections being raised by various states, including Pennsylvania, Massachusetts, New Hampshire, Virginia, New York, and North Carolina, over the absence of a bill of rights in the new Constitution, including some guarantee of religious liberty. To be sure, the original Constitution contained its own declaration of rights, at least eight or nine specific rights having been expressly addressed, including, among others: the guarantee of the writ of habeas corpus, the requirement that direct taxes be proportionate to population, the prohibition on bills of attainder and ex post facto laws, the right of trial by jury in criminal cases, limitation on convictions for treason, and the prohibition of any religious test for federal office. These rights, however, were not viewed as comprehensive enough to protect other rights demanded by the people.

The spelling out of other specific rights was originally regarded as unnecessary, to which Henry J. Abraham makes reference in his essay, "The Bill of Rights: Reflections on Its Status and Incorporation," (pp. 61-86) since it was widely held by the Founding Fathers that the national government of the new republic had no authority or power not explicitly conferred upon it by the Constitution. Alexander Hamilton expressed a view widely shared by his contemporaries, when he asked, "Why declare that things shall not be done which there is no power to do?" There were also those who shared the view that the mere listing of rights would run the risk of permitting infringement of those rights not spelled out in a bill of rights. This sentiment was later well expressed in the Tenth Amendment, which declares: "The powers not delegated to the United States by the Constitution, nor prohibited by it to the States, are reserved to the States respectively, or to the people." At the same time, there were those delegates to the Constitutional Convention who favored the incorporation of a bill of rights in the original Constitution. George Mason had remarked toward the close of the Convention that he "wished the plan had been prefaced by a Bill of Rights." It is noteworthy, however, that there is no indication of a single delegate who expressed opposition in principle to the adoption of a bill of rights.

Indeed, had it not been for the promise of the First Congress that it would complete the explicit guarantees of other civil rights, to be embodied in a bill of rights, the ratification of the Constitution might well have failed.[15] The first ten amendments, which make up the Bill of Rights, were designed in part "to quiet the fears" of those who might otherwise have opposed the Constitution in its original form.[16] The demand for religious liberty was understandably most vigorously expressed by religious dissenters, especially, Baptists, Deists, Methodists, Presbyterians, Quakers, and Unitarians, among others. Indeed, the churches were among the most vigorous advocates of what would become the religion clauses of the First Amendment. It should be noted, however, that by the time of the adoption of the Bill of Rights, twelve of the states had constitutions and all of them guaranteed religious liberty as a right, even though in five of the states provisions were made for the establishment of religion.

The first ten amendments to the Constitution, generally referred to as the Bill of Rights, were adopted by the Congress on 25 September 1789. Ratification by the states came within a little more than two years: New Jersey, 20 November 1789; Maryland, 19 December 1789; North Carolina, 22 December 1989; South Carolina, 19 January 1790; New Hampshire, 25 January 1790; Delaware, 28 January 1790; New York, 24 February 1790; Pennsylvania, 10 March 1790; Rhode Island, 7 June 1790; Vermont, 3 November 1791; and Virginia, 15 December 1791.[17] In contrast to the English Bill of Rights of 1689, in which the powers of Parliament are protected against the encroachments of the monarch, the American Bill of Rights was created to protect the individual against the intrusions of the legislative and executive branches of the government. As James Madison expressed it, "If we advert to the nature of Republican Government we shall find that censorial power is in the people over the Government, and not in the Government over the people." Nowhere in the Bill of Rights is this more sharply affirmed than in the words of the First Amendment: "Congress shall make no law respecting an establishment of religion or prohibiting the free exercise thereof; or abridging the freedom of speech or of the press; or the right of the people peaceably to assemble, and to petition the Government for a redress of grievances."

Although nine of the thirteen colonies had established churches, four did not (Rhode Island, Pennsylvania, New Jersey, and Delaware). By the time the First Amendment was adopted, however, only three states had an established church—Massachusetts, New Hampshire, and Connecticut. Of even greater significance is that no two states shared the same religious configuration with respect to its population. Not to be overlooked is that in the decade between the Declaration of Independence and the Constitutional Convention, numerous states had made declarations in support of religious freedom prior to the adoption of the Bill of Rights.

Numerous examples of the provisions for religious liberty may be found in the state constitutions and statutes themselves. In the "Virginia Declaration of Rights" of 1776, it was affirmed that "all men are equally entitled to the free exercise of religion, according to the dictates of conscience." In its final meeting under the state constitution, the Virginia Assembly affirmed, "That all dissenters, of whatever denomination . . . shall, from and after passing this act, be totally free and exempt from all levies, taxes and impositions whatever, towards supporting and maintaining the said [i.e. established] church."[18] In addition, "No man or class of men, ought on account of religion to be invested with peculiar emoluments or privileges, not subjected to any penalties or disabilities, unless under color of religion the preservation of equal liberty and the existence of the State are manifestly endangered."[19]

Delaware declared, "That all Men have a natural and unalienable Right to worship Almighty God according to the Dictates of their own Consciences and Understandings; that no Man ought or of Right can be compelled to attend any religious Worship or maintain any Ministry contrary to or against his own free Will and Consent, and that no Authority . . . shall in any Case interfere with, or in any Manner controul the Right of Conscience in the Free Exercise of Religious Worship." Admittedly, the declaration was limited to "all Persons professing the Christian Religion."[20]

Although generally limited to some form of the Christian religion, in the decade prior to the Constitutional Convention, various state constitutions provided guarantees for the rights of conscience and religious freedom. The Maryland constitution declared, "As it is the duty of every man to worship God in such manner as he thinks most acceptable to him; all persons professing the Christian religion, are equally entitled to protection in their religious liberty." The constitution further provided that the legislature may, "in their discretion," require a general tax for support of the Christian religion, for the support of any particular minister, denomination, place of worship, or for the benefit of the poor.[21]

The New Jersey constitution explicitly prohibited any person's being denied the right of freedom of worship, or being required to worship in any manner contrary to his "own faith and judgment," or being compelled to pay taxes for support of any religion or ministry contrary to his own beliefs. Any form of discrimination between the various Protestant sects was denied. The guarantees of religious freedom, however, were limited to Protestants.[22]

Similarly, the constitution of North Carolina affirmed that "all men have a natural and unalienable right to worship Almighty God according to the dictates of their own consciences," but limited this right to Protestants.[23] The Pennsylvania constitution affirmed religious freedom also as an "unalienable right," but did not limit this right to Christians, but rather to anyone "who acknowledges the being of a God."[24] Similar provisions appeared in the constitutions of New York and Vermont.[25]

Although with an established church, which would continue until 1819, the New Hampshire constitution of 1784 declared in the manner of other state constitutions already cited, that every individual has a natural and unalienable right to worship God according to the dictates of his conscience, and reason" and no person could be molested or restrained for worshipping God in accordance with his conscience. Furthermore,"no person of any one particular religious sect or denomination, shall ever be compelled to pay towards the support of the teacher or teachers of another persuasion, sect or denomination." Finally, it affirmed the equality of all denominations. "Every denomination . . . shall be equally under the protection of the law; and no subordination of any one sect or denomination to another, shall ever be established by law."[26]

The passage in Virginia in 1786 of Thomas Jefferson's "Act for Establishing Religious Freedom," a mere decade after the Declaration of Independence and a year before the Constitutional Convention and by an overwhelming majority, became the primary source of other state statutes and constituted the prevailing view of church and state at the time of the nation's founding. As Thomas J. Curry has shown, "Every colony-turned-state altered the Church-State arrangements it had inherited from colonial times."[27]

A primary reason for these declarations on religious freedom was that within the states as well as the republic at large religious diversity, not religious unity, characterized the life of the new nation. In the absence of any religious consensus among a population the vast majority of whom was unchurched—described "as the largest proportion of unchurched in Christendom,"[28] —assurances of religious liberty were needed to protect the rights of the religious diversity through prohibiting government intrusion in religious affairs. Such assurances of religious liberty, even if narrowly conceived, were an important way of building a consensus in the face of religious diversity and thereby garnering political support for the new state and federal governments. At the time of the ratification of the Constitution, fewer than 10 percent of the population were members of churches and synagogues and "in 1800 there were fewer churches relative to the population than at any other time before or since."[29]

The Constitutional provisions pertaining to religion were born out of both philosophical and practical considerations in an era that in so many ways is quite different from the present. It is important to remember that the First Amendment with its guarantee of institutional independence between church and state and its prohibition of government intervention in the exercise of religious freedom, for the most part, was not imposed upon the churches, but rather the churches claimed independence for themselves and, in the words of Winthrop S. Hudson, did so "for good theological reasons."[30] The churches saw their exercise of religious liberty to be a right unhindered by government interference or subject to government jurisdiction.

Today, there is a growing sentiment, which holds that the Establishment Clause is not to be directed toward independence between the institutions of church and state, and certainly not toward a "benevolent neutrality" between religion and irreligion, but toward non-preferential treatment of any particular church or religion. This requires not separation, it is argued, but accommodation and close cooperation between church and state, religion and government. The conflict between these two interpretations inevitably raises the question of original intent of the framers of the Establishment Clause. The debate has become particularly intense since the dissenting opinion of Chief Justice William H. Rehnquist in *Wallace v. Jaffree*, in which he declared, "There is simply no historical foundation for the proposition that the Framers intended to build the 'wall of separation' [between church and state]. . . ." "The 'wall of separation between church and state' is a metaphor based on bad history. . . . It should be," he said, "frankly and explicitly abandoned."[31] The debate over this interpretation of the Establishment Clause is critically examined historically by several of the essays in this volume.

At present, there is considerable pressure being brought to bear by some sectors of organized religion to secure the sanction and support of government in carrying out many of the church's ministries and programs. In glaring contrast to the latter part of the eighteenth century at the time of the adoption and ratification of the Bill of Right is the phenomenal rise in the status of church membership to approximately two-thirds of the total population. Organized religion today plays a prominent role in the body politic with respect to a broad range of political issues and in the political campaigns of candidates for public office. Recent American presidents have, in turn, encouraged and

welcomed the support of religious groups and pledged themselves to restore the values associated with traditional religion,
including support for prayer in the public schools and "equal
access" of religious groups to use public school facilities as a part
of the extra-curricular programs of the public schools. There is a
growing clamor today on the part of many within both
government and organized religion for accommodation and
cooperation between the institutions of religion and government
so long as the relationship is one in which there is nonpreferential treatment as between the various denominations.

The original essays which follow call the reader to review the
theoretical and historical roots of the Bill of Rights, with
particular focus on the religion clauses of the "First Freedom" of
the First Amendment, which has long been viewed as the cornerstone of America's Bill of Rights. The essays address a variety of
themes relating particularly to religion and the Bill of Rights,
including the theological sources as reflected in the Reformed
tradition, religion and ratification, bicentennial reflections on the
Bill of Rights and the incorporation of the religion clauses,
original intent and the Supreme Court today, original intent and
the historical quest for comparable consensus, and the unity of
the religion clauses.

From time to time, there is special need for a reexamination
of the Bill of Rights, both in its historical context and as to its
meaning and significance today. Perhaps that need has never
been greater than now, approximately two hundred years after
the ratification of the Bill of Rights, at a time when for many the
meaning of the First Amendment in American society is
questioned and appears to be in conflict with moral and
religious values that are advanced not only for the public square
but for the reshaping of America's nationhood. At such a time,
Americans would do well to consider the fundamental role that
the "First Freedom" of the Bill of Rights has played in both the
political and religious life of the nation, a role in which both religion and the state have been well served for two hundred years.

NOTES

1.   Samuel Eliot Morrison, *The Oxford History of the American People* (New York: Oxford University Press, 1965), 305. Thomas Jefferson, who was in France and therefore not one of the delegates, wrote to John Adams, 30 August 1787, that the Convention was "really an assembly of demigods"; see Julian P. Boyd, ed. *The Papers of Thomas Jefferson* (Princeton: Princeton University Press, 1950-), 12:69.

2.   Max Farrand, ed., *The Records of the Federal Constitution.* 4 vols. (New Haven: Yale University Press, 1937), 2:648 (17 September 1787).

3.   Quoted in Morrison, *The Oxford History of the American People,* 311.

4.   James Madison to Thomas Jefferson, 6 September 1787, *The Papers of James Madison,* ed. William T. Hutchinson et al. (Chicago: University of Chicago Press, 1962-1977, vols. 1-10; Charlottesville: University of Virginia Press, 1977- , vols. 11-16), 10:163-64. The final volume (17) is expected to be published in 1991.

5.   Robert A. Rutland, *James Madison: The Founding Father* (New York: Macmillan Publishing Co., 1987), 19.

6.   Ibid., 312.

7.   Isaac Backus, *A History of New England* (1774-75?); quoted in Anson Phelps Stokes, *Church and State in the United States.* 3 vols. (New York: Harper and Brothers, 1950), 1:307. Similar sentiments were expressed by John Witherspoon, Thomas Jefferson, and James Madison, among others.

8.   This lone reference to religion in the Constitution of 1787 is addressed in some detail in this volume by Edwin S. Gaustad in his essay, "Religion and Ratification," 41-59.

9.   Farrand, *The Records of the Federal Constitution of 1787.* 3:227.

10.   Joseph Story, *Commentaries on the Constitution of the United States: With a Preliminary Review of the Constitutional History of the Colonies and States before the Adoption of the Constitution.* 3 vols. (Boston, 1905), 3:1841; quoted in Philip B. Kurland and Ralph Lerner, eds. *The Founders' Constitution.* 5 vols. (Chicago: University of Chicago Press, 1987), 6:646.

11.   *McDaniel v. Paty* 435 U.S. (1978).

12.   Kurland and Lerner, *The Founders' Constitution*, 4:640.

13.   Debate in Massachusetts Ratifying Convention, 30 January 1788;
       quoted in ibid., 4:643.

14.   With the vote of New Hampshire for ratification, 21 June 1788,
       the Constitution was formally adopted; Rhode Island became the
       last of the thirteen states to ratify the Constitution, 29 May 1790,
       despite strong Anti-Federalist forces opposing ratification.

15.   Not all rights guaranteed in the Constitution are, of course, to be
       found in the Bill of Rights or the first ten amendments. In
       addition to the approximately twenty-four rights spelled out in
       the Bill of Rights, additional rights are guaranteed in the
       Thirteenth Amendment, the Fourteenth Amendment, the
       Fifteenth Amendment, and the Sixteenth Amendment, all of
       which have added substantially to the meaning and application
       of the American Bill of Rights.

16.   Edward S. Corwin, *The Constitution and What It Means Today*
       (Princeton: Princeton University Press, 1963), 188.

17.   One hundred and fifty years after their formal adoption the
       amendments were subsequently ratified by Massachusetts, 2
       March 1939; Georgia, 18 March 1939; and Connecticut, 19 April
       1939.

18.   Quoted in Stokes, *Church and State in the United States*, 1:304.

19.   "Virginia Declaration of Rights," 12 June 1776, Section 16.

20.   "Delaware Declaration of Rights and Fundamental Rules," 11
       September 1776.

21.   Maryland Constitution of 1776, Declaration of Rights, Nos. 33-36.

22.   New Jersey Constitution of 1776, Arts. 18, 19.

23.   North Carolina Constitution of 1776, Arts. 19, 31-32, 34.

24.   Pennsylvania Constitution of 1776, Declaration of Rights.

25.   New York Constitution of 1777, Arts. 38, 39; and Vermont
       Constitution of 1777, Ch. 1, Sec. 3; Ch. 2, Sec. 41.

26.   New Hampshire Constitution of 1784, Part 1, Articles 5, 6.

27.   Thomas J. Curry, *The First Freedoms: Church and State in America
       to the Passage of the First Amendment* (New York: Oxford
       University Press, 1986), 134.

28.   William Warren Sweet, *Religion in Colonial America* (New York:
       Charles Scribner's Sons, 1942), 334.

29.   George Dargo, *Roots of the Republic: A New Perspective on Early
       American Constitutionalism* (New York: Praeger, 1974), 89.

30.   See Winthrop S. Hudson, "The Theological Basis for Religious
        Freedom," *Journal of Church and State*   3 (November 1961):130-36.
31.   *Wallace v. Jaffree,* 472 U.S. 38 (1985) at 107.

1

The Reformed Tradition and
the First Amendment

DAVID LITTLE

To argue that there is an important, if subtle, historical connection between the Reformed tradition and the First Amendment is a challenging task. It is, to begin with, to fly in the face of certain fashionable beliefs about the rise of religious liberty in general, and, in particular, about the historical causes of the provisions for religious and other liberties guaranteed by the First Amendment of the United States Constitution.

As Quentin Skinner in his influential work, *The Foundations of Modern Political Thought*,[1] tells the story, present-day commitments owe very little to a principled belief in religious liberty on the part of our predecessors. Much more is owed to the effects of pragmatic compromise and mutual convenience, evident, for example, in the Edict of Nantes, which provided temporary peace, at least, between French Protestants and Catholics in 1598. Given the circumstances of the time, competing religious groups simply found it in their interests to submit to a system of toleration rather than to continue hostilities against each other.

No particular theory was needed to reveal where their advantage lay. If any principles about freedom of conscience emerged, they were more the result than the cause of compromise. For Skinner, that is typical of our entire modern experience.

In that spirit, a related kind of pragmatic interpretation is frequently applied to the First Amendment. Justice William H. Rehnquist, dissenting in *Wallace v. Jaffree* [2] from the majority opinion that upheld Jefferson's "wall of separation between church and state," contended that the amendment was the product of political compromise rather than determined conviction. When James Madison, primary author and sponsor of the amendment, took the floor of the House of Representatives on 8 June 1789, to advocate adoption of his drafts, he did so, as he said, "not because they are necessary, but because they can produce no possible danger, and may gratify some gentlemen's wishes."[3] According to Mr. Justice Rehnquist, Madison was thus speaking as a "prudent statesman seeking enactment of measures sought by a number of fellow citizens," rather than as a "dedicated advocate of the wisdom of such measures."[4]

In support, Rehnquist cites the familiar story of Madison's early resistance to the whole idea of a bill of rights, and his gradual, and somewhat half-hearted conversion to the idea in the interest of achieving ratification of the Constitution. The conclusion is that as Madison's motives were all political, it is a mistake to read any more than a very limited intention into the religion clauses of the First Amendment. They are aimed exclusively at restricting the federal government from creating a "national religion." They have no bearing at all on the practice of the states, and, accordingly, might well permit various forms of active cooperation between government and religion at the state level. In short, no grand and absolute principle of church-state separation underlies the amendment, whatever Madison, along with his friend Thomas Jefferson, may have had in mind in other connections.

Lastly, Father John Courtney Murray, in his justly famous volume, *We Hold These Truths*, partly anticipated Justice Rehnquist's view. "From the standpoint both of history and of contemporary social reality," Murray wrote, "the only tenable position is that the first two [clauses] of the first amendment *are not articles of faith but articles of peace*."[5] When American citizens affirm their allegiance to these clauses, they are not thereby committing themselves to any particular religious or philosophical doctrine. They may rather understand themselves to be submitting to a pragmatic agreement compatible with and indifferent among a wide range of divergent convictions.

Murray was especially eager to dispel the popular belief that Roger Williams, the seventeenth-century Reformed thinker and founder of the Rhode Island colony, played a significant role in the background of the First Amendment. Those who hold such a view mistakenly "stress the importance of ideological factors in the genesis of the American concept of the freedom of religion and separation of church and state," and so they single out for special attention a figure like Williams. For Murray, however, the reality is that Williams's ideas "had no genetic influence on the First Amendment. . . . Williams is therefore to be ruled out as the original theologian of the First Amendment."[6] And that goes for any other thinkers that might be mentioned. To repeat: We have before us articles of compromise, not articles of principle.

There is obviously some truth in these accounts—who can deny the place of compromise and the pursuit of comparative advantage in all human action? Nevertheless, the accounts are all seriously one-sided. This essay will attempt to demonstrate against Murray that certain principles nurtured and refined by the Reformed tradition, and particularly by Roger Williams, are in fact indispensable for understanding the First Amendment. Contrary to Rehnquist, this essay will argue that in regard to freedom of conscience, principles did matter for Madison, as for

Jefferson, whatever role pragmatic adjustment may also have played in formulating the Bill of Rights. If the author succeeds in these two efforts, that should provide some evidence toward modifying Quentin Skinner's general theory about the rise of modern beliefs concerning religious liberty.

Toward dismissing Williams as a formative figure, Murray cites the conclusions of Perry Miller, the distinguished colonial scholar, who lays it down that Williams "actually exerted little or no influence on institutional developments in America. . . ."[7] However, Miller does not argue to this conclusion; he simply asserts it. Considered against the evidence, it is an odd assertion, indeed.

Elsewhere, the author has endeavored to demonstrate that there are at least two important lines of connection between Williams and "institutional developments in America"— particularly the institution of the First Amendment.[8] There is the "Lockean connection": John Locke's letters on toleration and the freedom of conscience explicitly influenced the thought of James Madison and Thomas Jefferson, two founders who played such an important role in working out early legislative formulations of religious freedom. And Locke's ideas, in turn, are, with one or two exceptions, simply restatements of the central arguments in favor of freedom of conscience developed by Roger Williams in the middle of the seventeenth century, when Locke's opinions on these subjects were being shaped. Whether Locke consciously borrowed the argument from Williams is difficult to prove, but the "fit" is striking indeed. At the very least, the similarities between the two men are enough to establish common membership in a distinctive lineage of ideas.

In addition, there is the "Baptist connection": The role of the Baptists in the "mutual reinforcement that took place . . . between the struggles for civil and religious liberty"[9] at the time of the Continental Congress and the Constitutional Convention is well-established. What should be emphasized is the enormous

importance of Virginia Baptists in supporting the Virginia
Statute for Religious Freedom passed by the state Assembly in
1786, after an intense seven-year struggle.

The Virginia Statute is a central part of the background out of
which the religion clauses of the First Amendment emerged. It
was authored by Thomas Jefferson, and shepherded through the
Assembly by James Madison. Madison also wrote his famous
pamphlet, "Memorial and Remonstrance against Religious
Assessments," in 1785 as a means of reenforcing the statute.

A key figure in this story of Baptist agitation for religious
liberty in the eighteenth century was Isaac Backus, and, in turn,
Backus's links to Roger Williams were direct and avowed.[10]
Again, much of the argumentation in support of religious
freedom developed by Williams found its way into Backus's
influential pamphlets, revealing strong theological and
ecclesiological similarities between the two men. [11]

By means of the Lockean and Baptist connections, the single
most important and determinative contribution Williams made
to the articulation of the principles of religious freedom and
separation of church and state in late-eighteenth-century
America was his doctrine of the free conscience, and the web of
beliefs surrounding that doctrine.

There can be no doubt that the concept of the conscience and
its right to free exercise lay at the heart of the thinking of
individuals like Jefferson and Madison, thinking that finally
produced the religion clauses of the First Amendment. James
Madison opened his Memorial and Remonstrance with the
following words:

[W]e hold it for a fundamental and undeniable truth, 'that Religion or
the duty which we owe to our Creator and the Manner of discharging it,
can be directed only by reason and conviction, not by force or violence.'
The Religion then of every man must be left to the conviction and
conscience of every man; and it is the right of every man to exercise it as
these may dictate. This right is in its nature an unalienable right.[12]

[And he added]: If 'all men are by nature equally free and
independent,' all men are to be considered as entering into Society on
equal conditions; . . . Above all, are they to be considered as retaining an
'*equal* right to the free exercise of Religion, according to the dictates of
conscience.' Whilst we assert for ourselves a freedom to embrace, to
profess and to observe the religion which we believe to be of divine
origin, we cannot deny an equal freedom to those whose minds have
not yet yielded to the evidence which has convinced us.[13]

During debates on the amendments to the Constitution
protecting freedom of religion, Madison made a series of
proposals, including references to "the rights of conscience." For
example, his original suggestion for the First Amendment was
"The civil rights of none shall be abridged on account of religious
belief or worship, nor shall any national religion be established,
nor shall the full and equal rights of conscience be in any
manner, or on any pretext, infringed."[14] Significantly, Madison
also included a provision that would apply directly to the states
(though it was of course dropped): "No state shall violate the
equal rights of conscience, or the freedom of the press, or the
trial by jury in criminal cases."[15] This was, he said, "the most
valuable [guarantee] on the whole list." It was as important to
restrain state governments in regard to infringing the rights of
conscience as it was to restrain the national government.[16]

Evidence of this sort ought to begin to make one wary of
Justice Rehnquist's thesis that Madison took a thoroughly
unprincipled, merely pragmatic, attitude toward the First
Amendment, one that might, under certain circumstances,
regard with indifference arrangements between church and state
that compromised the equal rights of conscience.

Clearly, Madison's reservations about a bill of rights
protecting conscience and so on, which he certainly harbored,
had nothing to do with lack of conviction. He opposed a bill of
rights in 1787, because he considered it unnecessary and
ineffective, but worse, because he believed it to be a definite

threat to protecting basic rights. Freedom of religion, speech, press, and so on were *natural* rights, not rights somehow dispensed to citizens at the sufferance of the government. To include a bill of rights as part of the national Constitution, might suggest, Madison feared, that these rights were delegated by the government, rather than possessed inalienably by the people in the first place.

Therefore, when in 1789, Madison advocated his drafts of a bill of rights, "not," as he said, "because they are necessary, but because they can produce no possible danger, and may gratify some gentlemen's wishes," he had been persuaded, in part by correspondence from Jefferson, that a bill of rights would *not* likely threaten basic rights, as he had earlier thought. Thus, yielding to the strong desire for a bill of rights on the part of "a number of his fellow citizens" was, he came to believe after all, not too high a price to pay for gaining ratification of the Constitution. *In this case, it was principle that controlled compromise, not the other way around.*

Nor was Madison's proposal, mentioned above, to protect the right of free conscience against state as well as national government but an isolated illustration of his uncompromising devotion to the principle of free conscience. On the basis of his resolute commitment to the Virginia Statute for Religious Freedom—amply demonstrated both theoretically and practically—there is no reason to doubt Madison's strong commitment to the protection of religious liberty against *all* governments, and not just some.

Lastly, Madison's powerful attack on the Alien and Sedition Acts of 1798 (written but ten years after the adoption of the Bill of Rights), provides the final balance of evidence against the Rehnquist thesis. In his Report on the Virginia Resolution against the Acts, Madison mounted a sustained defense of the rights of free speech and press, rejecting the whole idea of seditious libel. Instead, he supported, in effect, the doctrine that only overt violence or the direct incitement thereof may permissibly be subject to coercive restraint by the state. To try, as did the Alien and Sedition Acts, to restrict by force the free expression of ideas, including open complaints against the government, is, at bottom, to violate the "liberty of conscience." "[I]t will be the duty of all, in proportion as they value the security [of the freedom of conscience]," Madison wrote, "to take the alarm at every encroachment on [the freedom of speech and press]."[17] In a word, the rights of free expression find their justification in the fundamental principle of free conscience.

It needs to be remembered that for both Madison and Jefferson the conscience is the "nerve-center," so to speak, of moral knowledge and deliberation, and, as such, constitutes the core of self-identity of each human being. Conscience and personal consciousness are deeply intertwined. This condition, of course, establishes the "equal rights of conscience." Any attempt to seize control over the operations of another's conscience, to decide for that person what is right and wrong, or what constitutes that person's spiritual destiny, is to subvert that other person by robbing it of its moral center. Thus, were the rights of conscience "inalienable." To tolerate the transfer or "alienation" of one's conscience into someone else's hands is tantamount to self-destruction. Applying that idea to the relations between citizen and magistrate, Jefferson asserted that "our rulers can have no authority over such natural rights, only as we have submitted to them. *The rights of conscience we never submitted, we could not submit.*"[18]

It is important to stress here that, as Jefferson suggested in the above words, and made even sharper in the Statute for Religious Freedom, conscience is understood to possess "natural" moral authority; it does not need specific religious or theological warrant. That means individuals are capable of recognizing and implementing, indeed they are expected to recognize and implement, at least minimally, the virtues of conscientiousness, regardless of their religious point of view. "Religion" and "morality" are in an important sense distinguished from each other.

In the same spirit, it is never an acceptable exercise of conscience to invoke a specifically religious warrant for coercing or controlling someone else's conscience. Just as force may not be used in initiating religious belief, religious belief may not be used in initiating force.

What is most important of all is that this way of thinking presupposes a *forensic image* or *model of conscience* that provided Jefferson and Madison with a framework not only for picturing the basic character of individual moral life, but also for conceiving of the essential purposes and organization of government.[19]

The conscience, after the fashion of the judicial or legislative forums of government, assesses the owner's actions and attitudes according to rules of deliberative procedure that attempt to ensure "judiciousness" or conscientiousness of judgment. A conscientious person, like a proper judge or legislator, strives for impartiality, sincerity, honesty, veracity, and accountability in evaluating one's past or in prescribing action for the future, just as one strives for courage in executing the decisions, against contrary temptations and pressures. On this view, to have a conscience is to be disposed, seriously and forthrightly, to practice critical self-examination and reflection according to "rules of correct exercise," rules of inner dialogue and deliberation that embody the traditional idea of the moral and intellectual virtues.

As Madison's words, quoted above, reveal, religion was thought to be of special relevance to the affairs of conscience, since religious beliefs and practices characteristically define at the deepest level one's basic values, convictions, and purposes. Unless one can independently reflect, inquire, revise, and reconsider in regard to religious matters, personal freedom in any recognizable sense is in deep jeopardy.

An implication of this view, drawn by Madison and Jefferson, is that the judicial and legislative bodies of any civil order—namely, the "outward forums" of government—ought, above all, to be designed and structured so as to respect, promote, and defend the "inner forum," the conscience.

That means at least two things. First, it means that there is assumed to exist a vital boundary between the use of force by the civil government and the exercise of conscience by the citizens of that government, a boundary, so to speak, between the "law of the sword" and the "law of the spirit." Though it may be difficult in practice to know exactly where that boundary falls, there is no doubt of the distinction in principle.

Second, it means that the virtues of conscientiousness—impartiality, sincerity, honesty, veracity, and accountability—must become the standards for the general conduct of government as for the particular activities of the judicial system, the legislature, and the executive. Moreover, special constitutional provisions will have to be created for encouraging both personal and civil conscientiousness. That is, of course, the burden of all of the First Amendment guarantees. The rights of freedom of religion, speech, press, assembly, and of the redress of grievance all, in concert, are designed to promote exercise of conscience in regard both to "personal" matters *and* to public or civil ones. These liberties encourage individuals and groups to call the government to account every bit as much as to call themselves to account.

As suggested above, the ideas of Jefferson and Madison concerning the conscience, and "First-Amendment matters," spring in a most important, if complex, way from the thinking of Roger Williams. Many of the theological convictions of Williams on the one side and of Jefferson and Madison on the other are of course very different. However, Jefferson's and Madison's way of understanding the conscience, as well as of drawing out implications for the civil realm, is deeply indebted to Williams, and to a venerable strand of Christian thought that culminates in

Williams. It is hoped that by lifting up and inspecting some of those connections, the background of the First Amendment will be clarified.

Surely, Williams ought to be given credit for definitively crystallizing the doctrine of free conscience and for trying to put it into practice against enormous odds in the Rhode Island colony, and for doing that in a way that provided, as Sydney Ahlstrom put it, "an important anticipation of later American problems and solutions."[20] Still, Williams hardly invented the idea. As he saw with uncommon acuity, the concept of a free conscience was deeply embedded in early Christian experience, and, thereafter, in Western Christianity as a whole.

To have distinguished sharply, as the early Christians did, between the gathered community of believers, on the one hand, and the civil or governmental community, on the other, was to have laid the foundations, quite innovatively, for differentiating between an inner and outer forum, between a law of the spirit and a law of the sword.

If the spiritual order was not coterminous with the civil order, and if Christians, therefore, ought not to be compelled by the government to join the church or to subject their affairs to direct civil control, then the way was cleared for a new independent sphere of authority set alongside civil authority. Furthermore, if in religious matters the last court of appeal was no longer the civil authority backed up by the use of physical force and coercion, then the new, independent sphere must be understood to function in a way that excludes physical force and coercion.

Consequently, as Christians came to understand it, the "law of the spirit" creates room for—indeed, places great emphasis upon—personal determination and decision in accord with standards and procedures that are internal to and in keeping with the "sovereignty" of all persons, rather than external to them and under the sovereignty of the civil order.

This is, of course, how the doctrine of free conscience fits in Christian history. There are rudiments of such a doctrine in Paul's letters, and Augustine, the scholastics, Thomas Aquinas, John Calvin, and the Puritans, along with many others, give it extended and serious attention. The basic idea, as suggested in earlier comments on Jefferson and Madison, is that the operations of conscience are inseparable from what it means to be a self, or to give expression to that self. Within certain limits, therefore, the conscience of each person must be given ample opportunity to perform. People whose consciences do not operate properly, who do not satisfactorily comply with the demands and virtues of conscientiousness—impartiality, veracity, accountability, etc.—are deeply deficient.

Though it does become muddled in certain ways, the heart of the doctrine of free conscience, as it develops from the early church onward, is that the only true religious faith is conscientious faith. That means two things: first, that a person must be given an honest choice among competing views, and must not be compelled or manipulated beyond one's will. There must of course be different beliefs from which to choose.

It means, second, that human beings must be understood to possess the capacity, *free of outside human interference or control*, to weigh, sift, examine, and determine among different beliefs in accord with the virtues of conscientiousness, and to have the capacity to do that *prior to and independent of* particular religious beliefs. If people were not understood to possess such a capacity, it is hard to understand why they should be left free to make their own decisions in matters of faith, rather than have decisions imposed upon them by "those in the know."

In other words, the doctrine of free conscience requires that human beings be assumed to possess at least some *moral* capabilities "naturally." That is, they must be regarded as capable of living up, to some degree, to the requirements of conscience—impartiality, honesty, accountability, etc.—in the process of arriving at "willing belief."

Now, this idea of free conscience is deeply embedded in the entire Christian tradition. However, so far as Williams was concerned, it is the Reformed part of that tradition that sets the context for elaborating the notion. Williams was, after all, a Calvinist, if a deviant one. On the Reformation Monument at Geneva, his figure appropriately stands to the immediate left of the first string of the Reformed team, Calvin, Theodorus Beza, Guillaume Farel, and John Knox. He shared Calvin's belief in predestination and in the centrality of scripture, and he correctly perceived that the doctrine of conscience lay at the foundations of Reformed faith and life.

Calvin himself, of course, was more conservative about the implications of the doctrine of conscience than was Williams. In that way, Calvin was like his followers in the Massachusetts Bay Colony, such as John Cotton, with whom Williams debated before and after he was banished to Rhode Island. It is obvious that Calvin would never have tolerated in Geneva the latitude of religious belief and practice that Williams permitted in Rhode Island.

Indeed, there are certain themes in Calvin's doctrine of conscience that appear to oppose Williams's emphasis on conscience as a forensic center of independent rational deliberation and determination. For example, when Calvin emphasized, as he did frequently, that the principal function of the conscience is to render human beings "inexcusable" before God, he appears to leave little room for a constructive role for conscience, based on some vestigial natural-rational capacity understood to be at least partially uncorrupted by sin. Moreover, if revelation of the essentials of faith is taken to be as unmistakable as Calvin at times assumes it is, there would seem to be less room for honest disagreement and diversity of belief and practice than Williams believed there was.

On the other hand, Calvin did not always speak that way. On occasion he invoked, "that common distinction between the earthly forum and the forum of conscience. While the whole world was shrouded in the densest darkness of ignorance, this tiny little spark of light remained, that men recognized man's conscience to be higher than all human judgments."[21] And at times he went quite far in picturing the conscience as an internal forum for rational debate as between, "some argument which we adopt . . . to defend a right course of action . . . we have taken, while on the other hand there are other [arguments] which accuse and convict us of our evil deeds. . . . [T]hese arguments of accusation or defense . . . are constantly operative in fulfilling their function in this life. . . ."[22] When, then, this forensic model is coupled with Calvin's inveterate and elaborate emphasis on conscience as a seat of sovereign freedom above and beyond not only "the tyrannies of men," but also beyond *all human laws*, "whether made by magistrate or by church," the foundations are laid for Williams's radical interpretation of the doctrine.

Williams was not, of course, alone in pursuing the radical implications of the doctrine; many medieval sectarians, post-reformation Anabaptists, and left-wing Puritans did the same, often paying the supreme price for their efforts at the hands of the associates and followers of more conservative theologians like Calvin.

What is novel and altogether revolutionary about Williams is that, unlike other radical Christians, he was presented for the first time with the opportunity of institutionalizing the doctrine to an unprecedented degree, of using it as a practical organizing principle for building a civil-ecclesiastical order that departed in substantial ways from existing patterns.

At the bottom of Williams's design for this new order was a provision for stringently curtailing the permissible use of force. While Calvin was distinctly uneasy either about enforcing religious belief and practice or about countenancing force undertaken for religious reasons, he did succeed in convincing himself that there were times when these things were necessary. In contrast, Williams resolutely anticipated the sharp dissociation of religion from force, as noted above, in the thinking of Jefferson and Madison. Just as force ought to play no part in inspiring and directing religious belief, so religious belief ought to play no part in inspiring and directing the use of force.

In this regard, Williams did little more than call up and apply a familiar and pregnant distinction in Western Christianity, and present also in Calvin's thought, between the two tables of the Decalogue. Commandments one through four were understood as the duties owed directly to God, and were therefore, in the standard terminology, the "religious" duties. Commandments five through ten, concerning theft, homicide, libel, etc., were duties human beings owed one another; they were designated as the "moral" duties.

Since the moral duties centrally prohibit offenses against the body—arbitrarily depriving someone of life or the means of physical support (property or reputation), engaging in unfaithful sexual activity, and so on, the tradition came to construe them as governing, to an important degree, what was thought of as "bodily" or "outward" behavior, and the core of the term "moral" came to be understood accordingly.

Now it appeared to Williams, as it had to many in the Christian tradition, that because physical force, too, was something bodily, something outward, it was at least apposite as an instrument for constraining the outward offenses mentioned in the second, or "moral," table of the Decalogue. It follows as a basic moral requirement that force ought to be organized, ought to be administered, so as to prevent and protect against arbitrary bodily injury, and similar offenses.

Indeed, such an idea well summarizes Williams's conception of what he calls the "law moral and civil." Government is morally required, in fact generally authorized by God, as a vehicle for organizing or regularizing the use of force by means of force, if necessary. "The world otherwise," wrote Williams, "would be like the sea wherein men, like fishes, would hunt and devour each other, and the greater devour the less. . . ."[23] That seemed to him clearly to be the import of Paul's defense of the

authority of governments, and of their use of force, in Romans
13. In short, for Williams, the "law of the sword" has a legitimate
place in God's design. And as the control of force—something
"outward"—is at the center of the government's function, so
government itself is properly thought of as an "outward forum."

At the same time, the role of government is severely
restricted. That role pertains to the "moral" table, but
emphatically not to the "religious" table. If the core of morality
pertains to preserving the material or outward welfare of human
beings, the core of religion pertains to their spiritual or "inward"
destiny. While the law of the sword can, up to a point,
effectively control moral offenses of the second-table sort, it
cannot reach and control the inner, spiritual life of human
beings. Properly understood, that life is conducted according to
the inner "law of the spirit," and must be so respected.

> To take a stronghold, men bring cannons . . . muskets, swords, pikes;
> and these to this end are weapons effectual and proportionable.
>
> On the other side, to batter down idolatry, false worship, heresy,
> schism . . . it is vain, improper, and unsuitable to bring those weapons
> which are used by persecutors—stocks, whips, prisons, swords, gibbets,
> stakes. . . . [A]gainst these spiritual strongholds in the souls of men,
> spiritual artillery and weapons are proper. . . .
>
> I observe that as civil weapons are improper in this business, and
> *never able to effect aught in the soul,* so . . . they are unnecessary. . . .[24]

One comes, then, to Williams's definitive notion of the "inner
forum," the conscience, which according to him, is set apart from
the outward forum of the civil order precisely over the question
of the use of force.

To begin with, conscience is, to Williams's mind, a
universally available "natural" capacity. It is frequently
distorted and dim, but, it nevertheless resembles a "tiny spark,"
as Calvin said, that dependably abides "while the world was
shrouded in the deepest darkness of ignorance." "[C]onscience

[is] a persuasion fixed in the mind and heart of man, which enforces him to judge . . . and to do so with respect to God, His worship, etc."

"This conscience is found in all mankind, more or less, in Jews, Turks, Papists, Protestants, pagans, etc."[25] The implication, of course, is that each person (whether Jew, Muslim, Catholic, Protestant, or individual of any other conceivable persuasion, including atheism [26]) must, above all, be left *free to judge* concerning religious (or irreligious) belief and the duties pertaining thereto.

Such a conviction presupposes that everyone, therefore, possesses a two-fold natural capacity. First, without reference to any specific religious belief, everyone knows enough to know that the consciences of others ought to be respected. In other words, with due reflection anyone can come to understand the inappropriateness of trying to direct the human mind and spirit by "outward" force and coercion rather than by "inward" appeals and reasons. To understand that is to understand how the mind and spirit are meant to operate; it is to appreciate that the law of the spirit is not reducible to the law of the sword. Accordingly, people can know enough naturally to restrain and organize force in keeping with everyone's rights to conscience and bodily protection, in keeping, that is, with the "law moral and civil."

There is a moral virtue, a moral fidelity, ability, and honesty, which other men (beside Church-members) are, by good nature and education, by good laws and good examples, nourished and trained up in, that civil places need not be monopolized into the hands of Church-members (who sometimes are not fitted for them), and *all others deprived of their natural and civil rights and liberties.*[27]

I ask whether or not such as may hold forth other worships or religions (Jews, Turks, or anti-Christians), may not be peaceable and quiet subjects, loving and helpful neighbors, fair and just dealers, true and loyal to the civil government: It is clear they may from all reason and experience in many flourishing cities and kingdoms of the world, and so offend not against the civil state and peace. . . .[28]

In fact, in support of his belief in the universal and natural availability of basic virtue and fair-dealing, Williams went out of his way to emphasize how much more civilized and humane were the "pagan, barbarian" native Americans he encountered and befriended than were the (allegedly) "civilized" English Christians who so aggressively took up residence in the New World.[29]

Second, on Williams's view of the conscience, everyone is assumed to possess potentially the requisites sufficient to come to a conscientious and honorable judgment "with respect to God, His worship, etc.," despite important divergences among different views. To hold, as Williams did, that "without search and trial no man attains . . . right persuasion," [30] is to affirm that human beings are equipped, in the first place, to conduct a judicious search and trial in religious matters, and thereby to work their way toward authentic willing belief.

It is also to affirm that a genuine search and trial—the prerequisite for the exercise of the conscientiousness—is impossible apart from a diversity of competing beliefs and practices. Unless one is called upon to face challenges of faith, to do that in a way that is truthful, honest, impartial, sincere, and courageous, one can never become personally accountable for one's beliefs and practices. And unless one exists in the midst of free and open religious diversity, the prospect of challenge, and therefore of the opportunity to cultivate the virtues of conscientiousness, is diminished.

For Williams, then, the most serious liability produced by the civil enforcement of religion is the corrosive effect upon the development of conscientiousness. When there is an attempt to compel belief by outward force, the conscience and its constitutive operations are simply bypassed. There is no personal act of assessing the merits of the case, weighing evidence, hearing arguments, soliciting contrary testimony, or assuming responsibility for the judgments involved. There is, rather, the encouragement of hypocrisy, of feigned belief.[31] And, as Williams reiterates again and again, hypocrisy "turns and dulls the very edge of all conscience either toward God or man."[32]

That hypocrisy, as the bitter fruit of enforced religious belief, enfeebles "all conscience either toward God or man," is, it should now be clear, the heart of Williams's basic message. It is not just that established religion impedes and perverts the achievement of conscientious belief in respect to God and His worship in the inner forum of each individual. It is also, and equally important, that, by extension, established religion impedes and perverts the achievement of conscientiousness in the conduct of civil affairs, in the outward forum. Enforced religion corrupts the enforcer every bit as much as it corrupts the victim.

In rounding out this sketch of Williams's seminal views, there is need to sharpen the specific role of Christian theological conviction in his general theory of free conscience. It is obviously essential to Williams's views, as it is essential to much of Western Christianity, that human beings be thought of as capable of moral reflection and action prior to and independent of any particular theological or "religious" beliefs. Otherwise, as has been shown, it is impossible to make sense of the way Williams developed and applied the ideas of conscientiousness. He clearly believed conscientiousness *was more likely to develop in both religious and in civil affairs if less reliance were placed on enforced belief*. There existed, Williams believed, a "natural" "law civil and moral," knowledge of which emphatically did not depend upon religious beliefs, but upon "reason and experience," as he frequently put it. To his mind, non-Christians, and even anti-Christians were, of their own accord, clearly capable of both discovering and complying with the basic moral duties of the second table, as well as coming to recognize and respect the vital boundary between the outward and inward forums.

Still, Williams was explicitly and resolutely a Christian believer, and it is important to register how his theological ideas fit into this picture. They do so as a complement and a supplement to his theory of free conscience. To Williams's mind, the heart of Christian revelation reenforces and illumines the forensic model of conscience and its civil implications.

I affirm that that state policy and state necessity, which (for the peace of the state and preventing of rivers of civil blood) permits the consciences of men [to be free], *will be found to agree most punctually with the rules of the best politician that ever the world saw, the King of Kings, and Lord of lords* . . . in comparison of whom Solomon himself had but a drop of wisdom, compared to Christ's ocean, and was but a farthing candle compared with the all and ever glorious Son of righteousness.[33]

The civil state is bound before God to take off that bond and yoke of soul-oppression and to proclaim free and impartial liberty to all the people of the . . . nations, to choose and maintain what worship and ministry their souls and consciences are persuaded of: which act, as it will prove an act of mercy and righteousness to the enslaved nations, so is it of a binding force to engage the whole and every interest and conscience to preserve common freedom and peace. However, *[it is] an act most suiting with the piety and Christianity of the holy testament of Christ Jesus.*[34]

'Tis impossible for [people] to maintain Christ by the sword, and to worship a true Christ! [It is equally impossible] to fight against all consciences opposite to theirs, and not to fight against God in some of them. . . .[35]

This idea of consonance between a system of civil peace based on freedom of conscience and a Christian gospel conveyed freely and in peace by persuasion, admonition, and example, rather than by force, expressed for Williams the only correct vision of Christian politics. Christ's coming did not, on the one hand, produce simply one more national or civil religion, one more instance, that is, of a civil order, like Rome or Judaism of the first century, dependent for its moral unity on a common political religion. But neither, on the other hand, did his coming abolish the state altogether, as some radical Christian sectarians believed. The effect of Christ's life and death was not to delegitimize altogether the civil use of the sword.

In contrast to both of these extremes, the cardinal political consequence of the event of Christ, for Williams, was radically to restrict the administration of force by reorganizing it in keeping with the theory of the free conscience, and with the development of the concomitant virtues of conscientiousness. That could be done only by *secularizing* the civil order, by severely delimiting the jurisdiction of the state in regard to religious matters. It could be done only by learning, as Williams put it, that the "power, might or authority [of particular governments] . . . is *not* religious, Christian, etc., but natural, human, and civil."[36]

Although the radical Reformed cast of Williams's thought distinguished many of his religious views from those of Madison and Jefferson, the general "fit" among the convictions of these three men concerning the idea and civil implications of free conscience is remarkable.

CONCLUSION

In case the point has been missed, these remarks are intended as a rejoinder to historicism, especially of the pragmatist kind, that is, historical study that explains ideas, beliefs, convictions, including those of a religious and moral sort, by reference to *pragmatic* as opposed to *principled* interests. At the beginning of this essay examples were cited of the conclusions of Quentin Skinner, Chief Justice William H. Rehnquist, and Father John Courtney Murray concerning various aspects of the development of religious liberty in the American tradition.

This essay has attempted to demonstrate, against Murray and Rehnquist, that principles do matter when it comes to understanding the context of the First Amendment. An attempt has been made to show that principles, particularly as interpreted and developed in the radical Reformed tradition, are crucial for grasping what Madison and Jefferson had in mind in drafting and urging its adoption.

If these conclusions, in opposition to Murray and Rehnquist, are correct, then it follows that one must begin to take a highly skeptical look at Quentin Skinner's general thesis about the rise of freedom of conscience in the West. It may just be that a certain lineage of ideas, such as has begun to be sketched here, is a good deal more important in understanding the American tradition than the admittedly pragmatic ideas about religious toleration found among the French Politiques who influenced the religious settlement achieved in France at the end of the sixteenth century.

Let it be understood, this writer does not disparage the importance of pragmatic accommodations in the making of history. As Max Weber said at the end of *The Protestant Ethic and the Spirit of Capitalism*, "It is, of course, not my aim to substitute for a one-sided materialistic causal interpretation of culture an equally one-sided intellectualist interpretation."[37] It is just that during these days the intellectual tradition needs to be upheld, and this has been the aim of the author in this essay.

NOTES

1. Quentin Skinner, *The Foundations of Modern Political Thought*. 2 vols. (Cambridge: Cambridge University Press, 1978).

2. *Wallace v. Jaffree*, 472 U.S. 38 (1985); cited by Harvey Poe, "The Relation Between Church and State in the United States," unpublished paper. The author is indebted to Harvey Poe for letting him look at an early draft of his referenced paper.

3. Robert A. Rutland, *The Birth of the Bill of Rights* (Chapel Hill: University of North Carolina Press, 1955), 173.

4. *Wallace v. Jaffree*.; cited in Poe, "The Relation Between Church and State," 11.

5. John Courtney Murray, *We Hold These Truths* (Garden City, N.Y.: Doubleday and Co., 1964), 65.

6. Ibid.

7. Perry Miller, *Roger Williams: His Contributions to the American Tradition* (New York: Atheneum, 1962), 29.

8. David Little, "Roger Williams and the Separation of Church and State," *Religion and the State: Essays in Honor of Leo Pfeffer,* ed. James E. Wood, Jr. (Waco, Texas: Baylor University Press, 1985), 3-23 (Hereafter cited as "Roger Williams").

9. Bernard Bailyn, *Ideological Origins of the American Revolution* (Cambridge: Harvard University Press, 1967), 268ff.

10. William G. McLoughlin, *Isaac Backus and the American Pietistic Tradition* (Boston: Little, Brown & Co., 1967), 128 ff.

11. Little, "Roger Williams," 11-14, 22 n.46.

12. James Madison, "Memorial and Remonstrance against Religious Assessments," *Papers of James Madison,* ed. Robert A. Rutland and William M.E. Rachal, 10 vols. (Chicago: University of Chicago Press, 1973), 8:299.

13. Ibid., 300.

14. James Madison, "Proposals to the Congress for a Bill of Rights, 1789," *Conscience in America,* ed. Lillian Schlissel (New York: E.P. Dutton & Co., 1968), 45-48.

15. Cited in David A. J. Richards, *Toleration and the Constitution* (New York: Oxford University Press, 1986), 115 n.62.

16. Rutland, *Birth of the Bill of Rights,* 208-209.

17. James Madison, "Report on the Resolutions," House of Delegates, Session of 1799-1800, *Writings of James Madison,* ed. Gaillard Hunt. 8 vols. (New York: G. P. Putnam's Sons, 1906), 6:401.

18. Adrienne Koch and William Peden, eds., *Life and Selected Writings of Thomas Jefferson* (New York: Modern Library, 1944), 275.

19. This model is essentially the author's own construction, though it is drawn faithfully from the tradition of reflection on conscience. It is developed in David Little, Abdulaziz Sachedina and John Kelsay, *Human Rights and the Conflicts of Culture: Freedom of Religion and Conscience in the West and in Islam* (Greensboro, S.C.: University of South Carolina Press, 1987).

20. Sydney E. Ahlstrom, *A Religious History of the American People* (New Haven: Yale University Press, 1972), 166.

21. John Calvin, *Institutes of the Christian Religion,* ed. John T. McNeill. 2 vols. (Philadelphia: Westminster Press, 1960), 1:iv, 10, 5; 2:1183.

22. John Calvin, *The Epistles of Paul The Apostle to the Romans and to the Thessalonians* (Grand Rapids: Wm. B. Eerdmans Publishing Company, 1976), 49 (Rom. 2:15).

23. Roger Williams, *Complete Writings*. 8 vols. (New York: Russell & Russell, 1963), 3:398.

24. Cited in Miller, *Roger Williams*, 131-32.

25. Williams, *Complete Writings*, 4:508-509.

26. See ibid., 7:181.

27. Ibid., 4:365; emphasis added.

28. Ibid., 3:142.

29. See Little, "Roger Williams," 19 n.11. Cf. Miller, *Roger Williams*, 60-71.

30. Williams, *Complete Writings*, 3:13.

31. Ibid., 78:181; cf. Little, "Roger Williams," 10-11.

32. Williams, *Complete Writings*, 7:181.

33. Ibid., 3:179; emphasis added.

34. Ibid.

35. Ibid., 4:515-16.

36. Ibid., 3:398.

37. Max Weber, *The Protestant Ethic and the Spirit of Capitalism* (New York: Charles Scribner's Sons, 1958), 183.

2

Religion and Ratification

EDWIN S. GAUSTAD

This volume addresses the significance of the First Amendment with respect to religion. An essential preliminary to that subject, however, is the role of religion in the drafting and in the approving of the Constitution itself. What deficiencies made the First Amendment necessary? What religious anxieties made ratification of the basic document itself problematic?

When in the fall of 1787 the freshly-minted Constitution was sent out to the people to win their approval or to suffer from their disfavor, many of the delegates who had been so busy in Philadelphia during the preceding summer held their collective breath. And for good reason. It was far from a foregone conclusion that the document would in fact be ratified. For one thing, some of the delegates elected to the Constitutional Convention had departed in disgust long before adjournment, convinced that the members had far exceeded their authority to revise the Articles of Confederation, and further convinced that a domestic tyranny threatened the thirteen sovereign states. For another thing, some of those who stayed around to the very end declined at the last moment to lend their signatures and their prestige to the finished product. And well beyond Philadelphia itself, groups and factions gathered to oppose what seemed to them not federalism at all but unchecked and vigorous nationalism.

More than two hundred years later, it is too easy to convince ourselves that the Constitution had a kind of aura of sanctity from the moment Gouverneur Morris completed his last stylistic touches. But of course neither respectful silence nor unanimous approval was expected or received. The extraordinarily close votes in Massachusetts, Virginia, and New York, to say nothing of the extraordinary delays in North Carolina and Rhode Island, demonstrate the controversial and contested character of the heated debates. The *Federalist Papers* which were written to persuade New York to vote in favor of the Constitution barely succeeded in their task; other heroic efforts, though none so enduring as that of James Madison, Alexander Hamilton, and John Jay, were called for in other states jealous of their long-practiced, hard-won liberties.

In all of this discussion and debate, to what extent were religious sentiments a factor? And to what extent did the Constitution itself arouse religious anxieties or allay them? In dealing with these questions, it would seem that the most logical place to begin would be with a careful examination of whatever the Constitution has to say with respect to religion. It turns out, however, that an even more logical place to begin is with what the Constitution fails to say about religion. For the most striking fact about what the Philadelphia delegates managed to produce in '87 is not the document's religious assertions but its religious silences. Two sorts of silences require comment.

First, the Constitution lacked any general recognition of the overarching Providence of God, any rhetorical or ceremonial flourishes regarding the author of our Being, the Architect of the Universe, the Laws of Nature that owed their existence to Nature's God. The late eighteenth century is filled with language of this sort, and nearly every state constitution drawn up after the American Revolution is likewise filled with such religious terms. But the federal document is not and we are obliged to try to explain why not.

At least three reasons may be offered for this strange, virtually anomalous silence. First, the delegates in Philadelphia had their hands full, almost too full, with the major task that they had taken upon themselves. They would gladly avoid, even ignore, the one subject that would inevitably delay them in getting on with the main business of creating an energetic central government. Second, the subject of religion could do more than delay, it could divide. The distinctive ecclesiastical traditions of the thirteen states meant that little common ground existed, that little hope of creedal uniformity could be entertained. Silence, if not golden, was at least prudent. Third, some delegates, highly suspicious of institutional religion that assumed too much political power, preferred to give no encouragement to those who would intermix the civil and the ecclesiastical realms. These persons sought a civil, even a secular frame of government. Together these three reasons seemed sufficient grounds for avoiding the subject of religion in the Philadelphia Convention; to the citizenry at large, however, those silences rankled.

Did not the framers recognize, many citizens asked, the fundamental link between Christianity and common law? Did they not acknowledge the necessary connection between Christian morality and political stability, between the "Supreme Dispenser of all good" and the fortunes if not the very survival of this struggling new nation? To a large number of Americans, these questions had so obvious an answer that the failure to address them in the document that they were being asked to ratify was at the very least a mystery, and, at most, a calamity. What would be lost, argued William Williams of Connecticut, if the Preamble to the Constitution began in some such fashion as this: "We the people of the United States, in a firm belief [in] the being and perfections of the one living and true God, the Creator and supreme Governour of the world, in his universal providence and the authority of his laws; [believing] that he will require of all moral agents an account of their conduct; that all rightful powers among men are ordained of, and mediately derived from God . . . in order to form a more perfect union &c. . . ."[1] Writing in February of 1788, Williams said he would vote for the Constitution much more readily and happily if only it had started out with language similar to that which he offered. He added, however, that he would probably vote for it anyway, despite this regrettable and inexcusable silence, because the Constitution at this moment in the nation's history was "too wise and too necessary to be rejected."[2]

Williams did not stand alone in his unhappiness over these grave silences. Nor did the ratification of the Constitution by the summer of 1788 put the matter to rest. In 1789 some Presbyterian elders vigorously complained to the newly elected President George Washington that the Constitution lacked all explicit acknowledgment of "the only true God and Jesus Christ, whom he hath sent." The unruffled Washington calmly replied that "the path of true piety is so plain as to require but little political direction."[3] Many Americans, however, did not see it that way. Indeed, during much of the nineteenth century, agitation continued to urge that some portion of the Constitution be amended or revised or rewritten in order to make the nation's religious allegiances unmistakably clear.

The National Reform Association, for example, thought that the consciences of the "Christian millions" had been violated just to placate the "infidel few." Under this Association's program, the nation's charter should begin in this fashion: "Recognizing Almighty God as the source of all authority and power in civil government, and acknowledging the Lord Jesus Christ as the Governor among the nations, His revealed will as the supreme law of the land, in order to constitute a Christian government, we the people. . . . " The spirit of William Williams lived on and would continue to do so even in the twentieth century as efforts were repeatedly made to give the title of "Christian nation" some official status.

The other Constitutional omission with respect to religion is, of course, much better known and is fully addressed in this volume: namely, the lack of any explicit guarantee for the rights of conscience or for religious liberty. Why this silence? One reason is that some thought that implicit guarantees were good enough: the broad purpose to "establish Justice, insure domestic Tranquility," etc., for example, seemed to imply the preservations of many rights and liberties, including those that pertained to religion. Others thought that liberties were best defined and defended at the state level rather than at the national level. Eight states already had their own declarations or bills of rights at the time of ratification: the remaining five could have readily drawn up their own. Besides, argued some federalists desperate to get the Constitution ratified, many complain against us that the central government intends to do too much, that it arrogates to itself too much authority and power. Here is a major issue, the federalists could contend, that we have left to the states; we have left it decentralized, truly federal, not national. Therefore, you who are concerned about the threat of national tyranny should brag on us, not condemn us. Still others argued that all rights not explicitly delegated to the central government did in fact still belong to the states and to the people. Liberties were not denied, but entrusted to those who had been defending them against England for generations.

This omission of a Bill of Rights was, however, a far more serious matter than the mere failure to express a national faith or trust in Providence. The whole Revolution had been about liberty, had it not? How could a fundamental frame of government be so careless, so negligent as to omit sure and certain guarantees of those rights for which brave men had died? Unless, perchance, such a government really did have in mind some limitation upon or diminution of those liberties. This anxiety permeated all levels of society and in some states became the immovable obstacle to ratification.

When James Madison sent a copy of the proposed Constitution to Thomas Jefferson in Paris, the latter objected first and foremost to the absence of a federal Bill of Rights, to explicit guarantees of freedom. And religious liberty was number one on the Jeffersonian list.[4] Liberty, in Jefferson's view, was too precious to be left to the whim of popular passions or to the shifting moods of easily swayed legislatures. Fundamental rights must be built into the very foundation of a government. When in Pennsylvania some twenty-three delegates to the ratifying convention voted against the Constitution, twenty-one of them signed a statement complaining that conscience had been granted no rights whatsoever in this federal document, no protection at all even for "those persons who are conscientiously scrupulous of bearing arms." In Pennsylvania, these delegates pointed out, "the rights of conscience were held sacred" even when "common danger" threatened all around and even "when outrage and violence might have been expected." Surely, the nation could do no less.[5] In state after state, delegates either swallowed hard over the failure to guarantee religious freedom (among other freedoms), or they refused to swallow at all. North Carolinians, for example, did not want to place bets on the future: they would withhold their approval of the Constitution until the First Congress did in fact draw up a bill of rights for the nation. And in Virginia, only the personal assurance of James Madison that he would make such amendments the first order of congressional business brought that state narrowly into the approving column.

Religious liberty was, of course, soon taken care of. Religious neutrality (or was it indifference?) was, however, another matter, not so easily remedied or repaired. Those who would make the case for indifference toward religion found their hand strengthened not only by what the delegates failed to do, but by what they managed so shockingly to assert. In Article VI of the

Constitution, the delegates had actually gone so far as to declare that "No religious Test shall ever be required as a Qualification to any Office or public Trust under the United State." No religious test at all? Did the delegates really intend that the presidential office, for example, be open to a Moslem, a papist, an infidel, or atheist? To ask the question was to reveal the dangerous absurdity of the provision—or at least many so argued as they found yet another reason to vote against ratification.

In the ratifying convention of Massachusetts several gentlemen argued that such strict religious neutrality represented a departure from the principles of that state's forefathers; moreover, the language of Article VI would permit even "deists, atheists, &c." to enter the general government, with the inevitable consequence that all public virtue would soon be at an end.[6] In New Hampshire, an Anti-Federalist pointed out that under these all too indiscriminate terms "we may have a Papist, a Mohomatan, a Deist, yea an Atheist at the helm of Government." Unlike any other civil government known to the Western world, the United States would not cherish its religious heritage, but totally abandon it. Is it "good policy to discard all religion?" inquired the aggrieved delegate. Public servants who had no regard for the laws of God "will have less regard to the laws of men, or to the most solemn oaths or affirmations." And so the New Hampshire polemic of 1788 concluded with the unspoken premise with which it had begun: "Civil governments can't well be supported without the assistance of religion."[7]

This central assumption was even more elegantly stated and persuasively argued in the pages of the *Massachusetts Gazette* as the moment for ratification in that state drew near. Our people, the author proudly noted, have stood for and fought for liberty. But it is just this love of liberty "that has induced them to adopt a religious test," for it is religion that "secures our independence as a nation." All nations acknowledged the need of religion; all, or almost all, instructed both old and young in those religious principles that had "a direct tendency to secure the practice of good morals and consequently the peace of society." Just as governments had a right to instruct their citizens in the arts of defense in order to promote external peace, so they had a right to instruct their citizens "in such principles as tend to secure internal peace." At an absolute minimum, the Constitution should be amended to exclude both "Papists and Atheists" from ever holding public office, the former because they acknowledged a foreign power, the latter "because they have no principles of virtue."

And if all this argument did not persuade, then the Massachusetts author played his trump card. We have an example immediately beside us, he pointed out, of a society that required no affirmation of or allegiance to religion: namely, the state of Rhode Island. There, as we all know, people "do whatever they please without any compunction. . . . they have no principles of restraint but laws of their own making; and from such laws may heaven defend us." How sad it was, this writer concluded, that here we are trying to create a new nation, trying to "build an elegant house"; yet, we deny ourselves the necessary tools to work with by trying to "establish a durable government without the publick protection of religion."[8] Maryland's Luther Martin, no friend to strong central government, sarcastically observed that in the Philadelphia Convention, some were "so unfashionable as to think . . . that in a Christian country it would be at least decent to hold out some distinction between the professors of Christianity and downright infidelity or paganism."[9]

A Pennsylvania critic pointed out in the fall of 1788 that all the world had found it necessary for the survival and strength of government to maintain some religious foundation. His words dripping with sarcasm, he then commented: "What the world could not accomplish from the commencement of time till now, they [the Philadelphia delegates] easily performed in a few moments." What he had in mind, of course, was the provision against any religious test. "This is laying the ax to the root of the tree," he added, "whereas other nations only lopped off a few noxious branches." But his objection was not so much to the religious test provision itself as to the removal of religion as one possible check upon a too strong central government. His Anti-Federalist bias came through clearly when he slyly noted that it must be only weak and feeble governments that require the sanction of religion. The proposed Constitution, on the other hand, envisions an "energetic" government; as such, it "disdains such contemptible auxiliaries as the belief of a Deity, the immortality of the soul, or the resurrection of the body, a day of judgment, or a future state of rewards and punishments." The aggrieved writer from Carlisle concluded that "the grand convention hath dexterously provided for the removal of every thing that has ever operated as a restraint upon government in any place or age of the world." Wise men, liberty loving men, will simply not vote for such an unchecked elevation of power, for such a frame of government that knows no law higher than itself.[10]

In New York, one "Cincinnatus" found even darker motives behind the provision for no religious test. Since the Constitution made no mention of liberty of conscience and since the only allusion to such liberty lay in this single sentence of Article VI, then one must conclude that no other such liberty is protected or will be respected. We must assume that all other conscientious behavior, religious or otherwise, would be regulated by the new federal government. "For, though no such power is expressly given, yet it is plainly meant to be included in the general powers, or else this exception would have been totally unnecessary."[11] Cincinnatus began his discussion by declaring that if men intended to vote for this Constitution, they should at least make some effort to understand it. And his understanding of what powers were reserved to the new government would, if widely shared, lead many to oppose ratification with all their might.

On the other hand, if persuasive arguments on behalf of religious tests could be offered, still more persuasive arguments could be offered against such tests. And even in a nation so largely Christian, so self-consciously Protestant, such arguments prevailed. Philadelphia merchant and later friend to Jefferson, Tench Coxe, in the fall of 1787 contrasted the liberality of the United States with the religious restrictions applied abroad. "In Italy, Spain, and Portugal," he wrote, "no protestant can hold a public trust." And in England, no dissenter from the Established Church can be elected or appointed to office. The Constitutional Convention "has the honour of proposing the first public act, by which any nation has ever divested itself of a power, every exercise of which is a trespass on the Majesty of Heaven."[12]

Connecticut's representative to the Constitutional Convention, Oliver Ellsworth, reviewed the way that religious tests had operated in England since Charles II, their baleful effect, their deceitful character (the law was imposed on the pretext of excluding "the papists, but the real design was to exclude the protestant dissenters"). When one sees how such laws have been used and abused elsewhere, one can only conclude, Ellsworth noted, that Americans would find religious tests "useless, tyrannical, and peculiarly unfit for the people of this country." Just as we would not submit to a test that would be in favor of Congregationalists or Episcopalians, of Baptists or Quakers, neither should we submit even to the most general kind of religious test. The first would be "indignity," and the second a sham. In England, Ellsworth reported, "the most abandoned characters partake of the sacraments, in order to qualify themselves for public employments." The only people excluded by religious tests were the honest and the conscientious, those who on principle would "rather suffer an injury, than act contrary to the dictates of their consciences." Religious test laws were mere "cob-web barriers," not to be relied upon, not to be erected simply for show. Happily in Connecticut,

Ellsworth concluded, we have no such laws; neither should the nation employ such a potential "engine of persecution."[13]

Consequently, in 1787 and 1788, many of those called upon to make up their minds concerning the Constitution found religion a sticking point. On the one hand, the document affirmed no faith; on the other hand, with its "no religious test" provision, it threatened to undermine the faith that did pervade the land: namely Christianity, and preeminently of the Protestant variety. Even some of the Constitution's supporters wished that the delegates had paid more attention to the religious language found in the states' charters. If the U.S. Constitution was a secular creation, hardly the same could be said of any comparable frame of government offered by the individual states.

In Pennsylvania, for example, to cite one of the more liberal states, religious liberty was—as one would expect—explicitly guaranteed. The Declaration of Rights drawn up in 1776 asserted that "no man ought or of right can be compelled to attend any religious worship, or erect or support any place of worship, or maintain any ministry, contrary to, or against his own free will." No surprise there. Somewhat surprising, however, was the following sentence that limited religious liberty to those who acknowledged "the being of a God," this limitation being a carry-over from William Penn's own time. Most surprising of all, however, was that the tolerant state of Pennsylvania did provide for a religious test for all its officeholders, and the test was even more restrictive than anything Penn himself had devised. In the same year that the Declaration of Independence was written and adopted, Pennsylvania declared that all legislators, before taking their seats, would solemnly take the following oath of office: "I do believe in one God, the creator and governor of the universe, the rewarder to the good and the punisher of the wicked. And I do acknowledge the Scriptures of the Old and New Testament to be given by Divine inspiration."

Such a religious test proved embarrassing to the resident libertarians and a cruel burden to those so summarily barred from civil office. In England the Unitarian minister and eloquent defender of American rights, Richard Price, complained in 1778 against Pennsylvania's restrictions in a state constitution that was "in other respects wise and liberal." Price predicted that this test would have a short life; even so, it reflected unfavorably, he argued, upon a whole people then engaged in a war for liberty, all liberty. Religious tests, Price added, "do inconceivable mischief by turning religion into a trade, by engendering strife and persecution, by forming hypocrites, by obstructing the progress of truth, and [by] fettering and perverting the human mind." Price also quarreled with those in his own homeland who, like the Archbishop of York, strenuously defended both the propriety and the necessity of imposing religious tests upon all potential office holders. What nonsense, Price responded. Politicians and statesmen have truly helped Christianity, he declared, only when they have opposed it, never when they have supported it. Political friendship had in fact, Price concluded, invariably "been almost fatal to it."[14]

In 1783 the synagogue in Philadelphia by public petition made obvious to all what would have immediately been evident only to a few: namely, that Jews by this requirement had all been barred from rendering that service open to all other citizens of the state. True, Jews in Pennsylvania in 1776 were few in number, the petitioners noted, but many were still fleeing the shackles of Europe for the enlarged freedoms of America. How unhappy it would be, they pointed out, if such a religious test would turn them away from Pennsylvania to some other state where "there is no such like restraint laid upon the nation and the religion of the Jews." Jews were as fond of liberty as were all their fellow citizens, the petitioners noted, and merely for doctrinal dissent they should not be excluded from the most important and honourable part of the rights of a free citizen."[15]

Leading non-Jewish citizens of Philadelphia agreed. Physician-patriot Benjamin Rush saw the restrictive test as a blight upon his own state in particular but upon all of the United States as well. When Benjamin Franklin became president of the state's executive council in 1785, Rush took hope, writing to Price that the prestige of the Franklin name added to that of Richard Price himself might be enough to "remove such a stain from the American Revolution." Then early in 1786, less than a decade after the religious test had been imposed, Rush happily reported to Price that the test law had been repealed, with the consequence that equal privileges were now conferred upon every citizen alike. This was only one more step, Rush noted, toward that grand effort "to enlighten and reform the world."[16]

In promoting a religious test (not in repealing it), Pennsylvania was more typical than exceptional. Massachusetts in adopting its constitution in 1780 provided for the "support and maintenance of public Protestant teachers of piety, religion, and morality." It also provided for all state officers to swear that they "believe the Christian religion, and have firm persuasion of its truth." Well, Franklin suggested in a letter to Price, it is necessary to remember how far Massachusetts has come from the days of fining, jailing, whipping, cropping, and hanging. So we have reason to hope, wrote Franklin, that the old Puritan state will keep striving for "greater Degrees of Perfection, when their Constitution, some years hence, shall be revised."[17] John Adams, on the other hand, saw no reason to abandon the "slender" establishment still preserved by his own state, predicting that such favoritism toward Protestantism "would endure as long as the solar system itself."[18] As things turned out, Franklin proved to be the better reader of portents and signs.

In the 1790s the newly admitted state of Tennessee determined to avoid the silences of the U.S. Constitution, now long in force, though it seemed, at first glance, to follow the lead of that federal document in its prohibition against any religious

test. In 1796 Tennessee provided that no elected official would
be subjected to a test, but at the same time and without a blush
the state declared that "no person who denies the being of God,
or a future state of rewards and punishments, shall hold any
office in the civil department of this State."[19] For a great many
Americans, not just in Tennessee, civil justice rested upon the
solid foundation of divine justice, even as civic virtue required a
divinely ordained scheme of punishment for the wicked and
reward for the righteous. This irreducible minimum of what
Franklin called "publick religion," Madison "national religion,"
and a later generation "civil religion" was widely cherished by
citizens up and down the Atlantic coast. And if such a religion
was necessary in settled and civilized communities of the East, it
was even more essential in the lawless and barbaric West.

In that connection it is instructive to look closely at how religion was viewed with respect to the West at the very time that
the Constitutional Convention was completing its important
labor. In that same summer of 1787, the Continental Congress
was busy setting long-range policy for the Western territories
and the subsequent admission of new states therefrom. The
document which ultimately emerged from these deliberations,
the Northwest Ordinance of 1787, had far-reaching significance
in many areas, of course, but examination here is limited to the
single facet of religion. Religion in this case, the subject of much
debate, exposed sharply divided opinions. While the Northwest
Ordinance did not have to be submitted to special conventions
of the people for ratification, it did have to pass the U.S.
Congress. And once more, religion proved to be a serious
stumbling block.

In Jefferson's 1784 draft of the Ordinance, religion was
conspicuous by its absence. Always reluctant to mix the
language of religion into instruments that had the force of law,
Jefferson—like so many of the framers of the Constitution
—preferred to avoid even the naming of the word. But this draft
of Jefferson's like that draft years earlier of the Declaration of

Independence fell into the hands of a committee. In 1785 Congress began to rework the Jeffersonian document which had temporarily been set into law. In March of that year, the Continental Congress recommended that the central section of every township be reserved for the support of education; then, the deliberative body added that the section just to the north be reserved for the support of religion. Charles Pinckney of South Carolina then proposed to substitute for the phrase "support of religion" this broader one: "for the support of religion and charitable uses." To some of the legislators, this looked like an improvement, but to others like a dodge. That troublesome word "religion," some argued, should simply be dropped altogether. Whereupon Pinckney withdrew his amendment, and Congress started all over again. How about setting aside a section of land that would be used just for "charitable purposes"? Four states were willing to support that proposition, but four votes were not enough.

But was not religion necessary in the West? Yes, most agreed. Well then, was not government obligated in some way to promote and support religion in the West? The answer to that more difficult question turned out to be "Yes and No," with the "no" votes sufficient in number to prevent that additional section of land from being set aside, even for "charitable uses." But the "yes" votes, or at least the sentiment behind those votes nonetheless won a partial victory in the final language of the Ordinance. Article Three begins in this manner: "Religion, Morality and knowledge being necessary to good government and the happiness of mankind. . . ." Thus far this was a victory for those forces wishing to provide some governmental endorsement of and perhaps assistance to religion. If they had been unopposed, no doubt this sentence in Article Three would have concluded in quite logical fashion by declaring that "schools and churches shall forever be encouraged." But too many delegates to the Congress were nervous about or baldly opposed to such a commitment on the part of the central government. So that famous sentence, though setting forth in its premise religion, morality, and education as a trinity of essentials, concluded much more lamely that "schools and the means of education shall forever be encouraged." This Ordinance, of course, also provided for the protection of religious liberty, but that occasioned no protracted discussion, no complex parliamentary maneuvering. In 1787 religious liberty was not the issue. Religious affirmations were an issue, and religious assistance, even of a generalized, non-sectarian sort, was still more a matter of controversy, debate, and ultimate defeat.[20]

A single sentence in the Northwest Ordinance thus summarizes the nature of a people divided on the question of what their government could or should do concerning religion in general or Christianity in particular. Religion and morality were necessary to good government and human happiness. Therefore . . . , what? Responsible authorities found themselves trapped in a cruel dilemma, or traveling down a passage that offered no exit. Older states had a special responsibility for and special anxiety concerning newer states; yet so far as Christian nurture or Christian virtue went, severe limits bound them and frustrated them.

In the state constitutions, one found much more readiness to affirm a faith, require an oath, or preserve a tradition. Yet, one did not find uniformity in the faith affirmed or protected, nor did one find all citizens resting easily with doctrinal tests and creedal assumptions. Nonetheless, if the union consisted mainly of states that declared their Christian faith, was not the entity which resulted from this combination of states properly called a "Christian nation"? Many thought it only axiomatic, self-evident if you will, that the whole was equal to the sum of its parts.

The Constitution's framers, on the other hand, knew that they walked a tightrope. They knew that the religious diversity represented by, say Connecticut, New York, and South Carolina, could not readily be encompassed in language of sufficient generality as still to permit some meaning. They knew further that consciences were tender, often rubbed raw by the practiced cruelties of earlier times. They also knew that dissenters against America's own ecclesiastical establishments stood ready to protest at the first sign of governmental favor or privilege. And finally, they knew that some in their midst believed that religion did not need and perhaps did not deserve any constitutional endorsement. The delegates even declined to offer public prayers, though the patriarchal Franklin tried to shame them into doing so after they had spent four or five weeks groping "in the dark to find Political Truth." Without divine assistance, Franklin observed, "We shall succeed in this political Building no better than the Builders of Babel." Franklin, of course, spoke only of those weeks spent in drafting a political document, but many throughout the nation thought his words equally applicable to the charter itself. We prayed for God's help in this very room during the Revolution, Franklin noted; we should pray for it now. And the Constitution itself, many would later argue, should also indicate its reliance upon that same "superintending Providence," that God who, as Franklin declared, "governs in the Affairs of Men."[21]

Thus, one observes the tensions with which the fundamental charters of states, of territories, and of nation are filled, tensions that remain obvious in the nation today. One Anti-Federalist of 1788, after reviewing the contradictions and confusions in 1787 and beyond, concluded that perhaps the only safe path was to rely more on principles than on precedents. James Madison would have heartily agreed. "It is safer to trust the consequences of a right principle," he wrote in his retirement at Montpelier, "than reasonings in support of a bad one." Precedent and tradition may have pointed to a "Christian nation." Principle, on the other hand pointed to a land that would be (to cite Madison again) "an Asylum to the persecuted and oppressed of every Nation and Religion."[22]

NOTES

1. Paul L. Ford, *Essays on the Constitution of the United States* (New York: Burt Franklin, 1970 [1892]), 208-9.
2. Ibid.
3. Paul F. Boller, Jr., "George Washington and Religious Liberty," *William and Mary Quarterly* 8 (October 1960):501.
4. Edwin S. Gaustad, *Faith of Our Fathers: Religion and the New Nation* (San Francisco: Harper & Row Publishers, 1987), 43-4. See all of Chapter 3 for a detailed treatment of Jefferson's and Madison's views on religious liberty.
5. Merrill Jensen, ed., *Ratification of the Constitution of the United States*, 7 vols. (Madison: State Historical Society of Wisconsin, 1976), 2:638.
6. Philip B. Kurland and Ralph Larner, *The Founder's Constitution*, 5 vols. (Chicago: University of Chicago Press, 1987), 4:642-3.
7. Herbert J. Storing, ed., *The Complete Anti-Federalist*, 7 vols. (Chicago: University of Chicago Press, 1981), 4:242. Also see Storing for Richard Henry Lee's explanation to James Madison concerning the absolute necessity of retaining a public religion as" the guardian of morals" (1:22).
8. Ibid., 4:247-8.
9. Ibid., 2:75.
10. Ibid., 3:206-7.
11. Ibid., 6:14.
12. Paul L. Ford, *Pamphlets on the Constitution of the United States* (New York: De Capo Press, 1968 [1888]), 146.
13. Ford, *Essays on the Constitution*, 167-71.
14. Bernard Peach, ed., *Richard Price and the Ethical Foundations of the American Revolution* (Durham, N.C.: Duke University Press, 1979), 54-55n. See also, p. 200 and all of Appendix Five.
15. Anson Phelps Stokes, *Church and State in the United States*, 3 vols. (New York: Harper & Brothers, 1950), 1:288.
16. Lyman H. Butterfield, ed., *Letters of Benjamin Rush*, 2 vols. (Princeton: Princeton University Press, 1951),1: 385-86. At this point, however, Pennsylvania had retreated only to the extent of not requiring one to declare belief in both the Old and the New Testaments. The other requirements of belief in God and in cosmic rewards or punishments remained.

17. Leonard W. Labaree, ed., *The Papers of Benjamin Franklin*, 14 vols. (New Haven: Yale University Press, 1965), 8:153-54.

18. Charles F. Adams, ed., *The Works of John Adams*, 8 vols. (Boston: C.C. Little and J. Brown, 1850), 2:398-99.

19. Gaustad, *Faith of our Fathers*, 172-73.

20. For a more extensive discussion of these negotiations, see ibid., 151-6.

21. Albert H. Smyth, ed., *Writings of Benjamin Franklin*, 10 vols. (New York: Macmillan and Co., 1905-07), 9:600-1.

22. For Madison's "Detached Memoranda" written in retirement, see Elizabeth Fleet, ed., in *William and Mary Quarterly* 3 (October 1946):554-56; for the "Memorial and Remonstrance" from which the final quotation is taken, see William T. Hutchinson, ed., *The Papers of James Madison*, 10 vols. (Chicago: University of Chicago Press,1962-77), 8:298-304.

3

The Bill of Rights: Reflections on Its Status and Incorporation

HENRY J. ABRAHAM

Americans may rightly view the ratification of the Bill of Rights—the first ten amendments to the Constitution—by the then requisite eleven states on 15 December 1789, with Virginia the eleventh and key state to vote affirmatively on that day, with genuine pride. The American Bill of Rights not only lives in its application to both federal *and* state levels of government, it does so in excellent health. It is in good hands under the aegis of the judicial guardianship to which our evolving constitutional firmament has assigned it, even if more implicitly than explicitly. Assuredly, it represents a guardianship that enables us to sleep far more soundly and contentedly than if that guardianship were lodged in the hands of either, or both, of the executive and legislative branches—for they are all-too-close to the endemic transcience of political passion and partisan division. *Pace* the arguably defensible negativism of such influential segments of

the quotidian scene as that of academe—which is prone to
develop guilt complexes with cheery alacrity on a perpetual
Yom Kippur scale—and that of the ubiquitous printed and
electronic media. Fundamental civil rights and liberties in the
United States are contemporarily more pronounced and more
secure than ever under our constitutional constellation. For that
demonstrable fact of societal *cum* institutional life and law, "We-
the-People," who, necessarily eschewing potentially deadly
complacency, have manifested a natural commitment to the
hallowed responsibility of embracing eternal vigilance as the
price of our freedom—"We-the-People" owe an abiding debt to
our judiciary, with the Supreme Court of the United States and
its awesome power of judicial review at its apex. In the 1955
Godkin Lectures, which he was preparing to deliver at Harvard
University when death intervened—and which his son then
presented for him as a poignant tribute—Justice Robert H.
Jackson expressed this conviction eloquently and ably: "The
people have seemed to feel that the Supreme Court, whatever its
defects, is still the most detached, dispassionate, and trustworthy
custodian that our system affords for the translation of abstract
into concrete constitutional commands."[1]

Professor Robert Allen Rutland has told the story of the birth
of the Bill of Rights over the memorable fifteen-year period from
1776 to 1791 with historical acumen, profound insight, and
uncommon clarity in his volume, *The Birth of the Bill of Rights*.[2]
It would be tautological to rechronicle it here. He succeeded
admirably in relating how Americans came to rely on legal
guarantees for their personal freedom; that the English common
law, colonial charters, legislative enactments, and a variety of
events in the thirteen colonies were the chief elements
contributing to the basic rationale for a bill of rights. But to
create the latter was far from the presumably facile task, viewed
by some rather naively as all but unanimously pre-ordained.
Much opposition abounded—initially perhaps surprisingly
embraced by leading Virginia Founding Fathers—largely

bottomed on the belief by a good many that a bill of rights was simply unnecessary; that the states, after all, had their own bills of rights; and that the body of the Constitution, as it finally surfaced on 17 September 1787 upon the conclusion of the Constitutional Convention's deliberations down on Fifth and Chestnut Streets in Philadelphia, contained ample safeguards against national (federal) mischief. Yet, ultimately persuaded by that trio of noble Virginians, Thomas Jefferson, James Madison, and George Mason—who had labored mightily to convince themselves of its wisdom—what is known today as the 462-word Bill of Rights, comprising the first eight articles of amendment to the basic document (or ten to some who prefer to include Amendments Nine and Ten) was born and submitted to the First Congress for its approval in April 1789. It was the young but politically savvy James Madison, member of Congress from Virginia, who had just defeated his friend and colleague for the post—as its effective floor manager. George Mason, it ought to be noted, had voted against ratification of the Constitution in the Virginia Constitutional Convention largely, albeit not exclusively, because of the absence of a bill of rights. On 25 September 1789, Congress sent twelve amendments to the states for ratification as the Bill of Rights, but two proved to be sharply controversial and failed of adoption (one calling for a fixed schedule of apportionment of House of Representative legislators, the other dealing with altering the pay of members of Congress. In retrospect, perhaps their adoption might have spared Americans some controversy).

Fully alive now to the need for its approval, Jefferson had written to Madison in March 1789, "The Bill of Rights is necessary because of the legal check which it puts into the hands of the judiciary." What he meant was a legal check against the *national* government—he was not worried greatly about the states since they had their own bills of rights, restrictions that the framers considered comfortably satisfactory. The central government, however, was a different matter, and there is

simply no doubt, whatever, that the overriding reason for the
Virginians' authorship and sponsorship of the federal Bill of
Rights was to place demonstrably far-reaching restraints on the
fledgling central government. Indeed, the very first phrase of
Article One of the approximately twenty-five assorted rights to
be found in the Bill of Rights reads: *"Congress* shall make no law.
. . . " Although the noun "congress" reappears nowhere in the
remainder of the eight articles that comprise the document at
issue, the latter was unquestionably intended to be applicable
against the national government only. Certainly that was the
understanding with which the eleven states ratified the Bill of
Rights—although Madison would soon come to believe that,
once having become the law of the land, it ought to be applied
against the states as well as against the national government.
James Madison would soon be joined by elements of the
propertied community who advanced similar contentions.

But, and one might well say, appropriately, it would fall to
the fourth chief justice, another renowned Virginian, John
Marshall, to be the first to adjudicate the question when, in 1833,
in the thirty-third of his thirty-four years on the Court, he
authored the Court's landmark opinion in *Barron v. Baltimore*.[3]
As was the case with the vast majority of the great nationalist's
plethory of opinions, he spoke for an unanimous tribunal in
ruling that the Bill of Rights applied only against the national
government, emphatically *not* against the states. His holding
commenced a history of litigation on the question of the Bill of
Right's applicability that, arguably, has never really been wholly
settled. To all intents and purposes, however, it was the first
section of the Fourteenth Amendment, which became part and
parcel of the Constitution in 1868, whose "due process of law"
and "equal protection of the laws" clauses would much later
provide the Court, largely due to the intellectual leadership of
Justice Hugo L. Black in the 1940s, 1950s, and 1960s, with the
tools to refashion constitutional law so as to apply the Bill of

Rights to the states—a process variously known as "incorporation," "absorption," or "nationalization."

The basis for the litigation in *Barron v. Baltimore* was laid
when the City of Baltimore, Maryland, began to pave some of its
streets. In so doing its engineers found it necessary to divert
several streams from their natural courses; near one, Barron's
Wharf, this resulted in deposits of gravel and sand which filled
up the channel and prevented the approach of vessels. John
Barron's fine wharf, previously the one with the deepest water in
the harbor, was thus turned into little more than a useless inlet.
Not amused, Mr. Barron obtained eminent legal counsel and
went to court (as all good persons did then and do now, true to
Alexis de Tocqueville's prescient predictions). He alleged that
Baltimore's actions had violated that clause of the Fifth
Amendment of the United States Constitution, which expressly
proscribes the taking of private property "for public use without
just compensation." Although Barron won his argument at the
level of the state trial court, which awarded him $4500 in
damages, his joy was short-lived. Baltimore appealed the
verdict to the Maryland State Court of Appeals, which reversed
the decision. The unhappy Barron then appealed this case to the
United States Supreme Court on a writ of error.

Marshall announced that "the question thus presented is, we
think, of great importance, but not of much difficulty." In a
handful of pages he demolished Barron's fundamental
contention that whatever is forbidden by the terms of the Fifth
Amendment of the national government is also forbidden to the
states and that the Court therefore has an obligation to construe
the Fifth's "guarantee in behalf of individual liberty" as a
restraint upon *both* state and national governments. The Chief
Justice's response was phrased in historical and constitutional
terms:

The Constitution was ordained and established by the people of the
United States for themselves, for their own government, and not for the

Government of the individual States. Each State established a Constitution for itself, and, in the Constitution, provided such limitations and restrictions on the powers of its particular government as its judgment indicated. The people of the United States framed such a government for the United States as they supposed best adapted to their situation, and best calculated to promote their interests. The powers they conferred on the government were to be exercised by itself; and the limitations on power, if expressed in general terms, are naturally, and, we think, necessarily applicable to the government created by the instrument. They are limitations of power granted in the instrument itself; not of distinct governments, framed by different persons and for different purposes.

If these propositions be correct, the fifth amendment must be understood as restraining the power of the general government, not as applicable to the States. In their several constitutions they have imposed such restrictions on their respective governments as their own wisdom suggested, such as they deemed most proper for themselves. It is a subject on which they judge exclusively, and with which others interfere no further than they are supposed to have a common interest.

. . . .

These amendments [the Bill of Rights] contain no expression indicating an intention to apply them to the state governments. This court cannot so apply them. . . .

. . . This court . . . has no jurisdiction of the cause; and [it] is dismissed.[4]

Marshall had spoken, Barron had lost, and the Court's unanimous opinion that there was "no repugnancy between the several acts of the general assembly of Maryland . . . and the Constitution of the United States," became the law of the land. Citizens like Barron were destined to have no further recourse until the ratification in 1868 of the Fourteenth Amendment, probably the most controversial, and certainly the most litigated, of all amendments adopted since the birth of the Republic. And be it noted that today, more than one hundred fifty years later, a live argument still rages whether Marshall's position is not in fact still the proper interpretation of the Constitution, regardless of the Fourteenth Amendment. That, for example, was the Reagan administration's position, giving rise to a rather fascinating—and sometimes rather silly—debate on the matter of the Constitution's "original intent" and its interpretative obligations.

What, then, of the Fourteenth Amendment? In and of itself it did not overturn the *Barron* precedent; it contains no such *explicit* purpose or language, and disagreement that, as indicated, persists regarding the intentions of the framers, particularly as to the extent, if any, of the Amendment's application to the several states. But certain evidence does exist and merits close examination.

The *facts* surrounding the proposal and passage of the Fourteenth Amendment in the Thirty-ninth Congress (1865-67)—led by the Radical Republicans and their Committee of Fifteen—are fewer than the resultant conjectures and analyses. It is known, however, that the 52 United States Senators (42 Republicans and 10 Democrats) and 191 Representatives (145 Republicans and 46 Democrats) wanted to do something to ameliorate the lot of the now emancipated blacks; that *de minimis*, they intended to embody the provisions of the Civil Rights Act of 1866, forbidding "discrimination in civil rights or immunities . . . on account of race" in the Amendment—although *political* rights were excluded from that understanding, because "*civil* rights" were designed to relate to personal security and personal property only; that at least to some extent, they were concerned with civil rights generally; and that they were interested in extending increased protection to property as well as to human rights, with the noun "person" soon to be applied to corporations as well. The Amendment was intended to remedy the lack of a "citizenship" clause in the original Constitution—and the initial sentence of the first of its five sections makes this clear: "All persons born or naturalized in the United

States, and subject to the jurisdiction thereof, are citizens of the United States and of the state wherein they reside." This, of course, would include blacks. Additionally, the language of the Amendment's last section, number 5, indicates some intention to provide Congress with the necessary power, if not the tools, to enforce the provisions of the Amendment: "The Congress shall have power to enforce, by *appropriate legislation*, the provisions of this article." That authority would become a major tool with the dawning of the civil libertarian revolution as of the 1960s.

Likewise, it is known that, unlike the Privileges or Immunities and Due Process Clauses, the Equal Protection Clause of the Amendment had no antecedent meaning but originated in the committee that drafted it—which could hardly have foreseen its subsequent controversial history and judicial application. And finally, it is known that with respect to the matter of the reach of the Bill of Rights, both the heart and greatest source of confusion and controversy of the famed Amendment is the well-known phrasing of the second, lengthy sentence of Section 1, which was composed chiefly by Republican Representative John A. Bingham of Ohio:

No State shall make or enforce any law which shall abridge the privileges or immunities of citizens of the United States; ["a fetus is not a person," intoned Justice Blackmun in *Roe v. Wade* in 1973, whereas corporations had been declared "persons" in 1886] *nor shall any State deprive any person of life, liberty, or property, without due process of law*; nor deny to any person within its jurisdiction the equal protection of the laws.[5]

There is no disagreement that the second phrase, which was lifted verbatim from the language of the Fifth Amendment, thus was intended to provide guarantees against *state* infringement supplemental to the Fifth's mandate against federal infringement. What does cause major disagreement, however, can be illustrated by two questions: first, *did* the framers of the

Amendment intend to "incorporate" or "nationalize" or "absorb" or "carry over" the entire Bill of Rights through the wording of its Due Process Clause, thereby making it applicable to the several states; and second, regardless of their intention, *should* the Bill of Rights be applied to the states, in view of the nature of the rights involved and the demands of contemporary American society. Again, it remains a live issue, although it may well be an academic one today, given the reality of the all but total incorporation of the Bill of Rights.

The Fourteenth Amendment was passed by Congress on 16 June 1866, ratified by the required three-fourths of the states—ten of these then being Southern Reconstruction governments which complied under duress—and it was ultimately proclaimed in effect on 28 July 1868. As a condition of their readmission to the Union, Congress had required ratification of the Amendment and extension of the suffrage to adult males "of whatever race, color, or previous condition." (The late Senator James O. Eastland of Mississippi was fond of calling it "that unconstitutional Amendment.") The Amendment had significant political overtones, for it was the key plank of the first Reconstruction platform drafted by the Radical Republicans, led by Thaddeus Stevens of Pennsylvania, Roscoe Conkling of New York, and George Boutwell of Massachusetts. In fact, the Amendment's passage by Congress in June provided the Radical Republicans with a welcome, ready-made campaign issue for the November 1866 election campaigns. Attention directed to the Amendment was almost wholly concerned with the political implications of bestowing full citizenship upon blacks. But there is no record of any campaign discussion or analysis of the matter of the application of the Bill of Rights to the states via its Due Process Clause or any other clause. There was much talk of the Amendment giving teeth to the Thirteenth Amendment and securing what the recent convert to the Republican aisle, representative Lyman Trumbull of Illinois, called the "fundamental rights and fundamental freedoms of all men."

Because of continuing disagreements on the "intent" of the Amendment's framers, some argue that their intent no longer matters, for the "felt necessities of the time" (Justice Oliver Wendell Holmes's celebrated, albeit often misinterpreted, phrase) and the inevitable growth of the Constitution, may *a fortiori* dictate the application of the Bill of Rights to the several states regardless of the Framers' intention. However, since it is preferable to have historical data to back one's contentions, both the proponents and opponents of total or even partial incorporation continue to invoke history to this day. As Holmes put it in his famed aphorism, "A page of history is worth more than a volume of logic." A great deal of published research on historical justification is available, yet there is no conclusive answer, for the evidence is not persuasive.

Originally, those *opposing* the incorporation interpretation enjoyed a slight edge. Briefly, on the one hand, they contended that had the framers of the Fourteenth Amendment intended to "incorporate" or "carry over" or "nationalize" the Bill of Rights to the states, *they would have written so specifically rather than rest on the general language of the Due Process Clause* or either of the two other mandate clauses in Section 1 of the Fourteenth Amendment. The *proponents*, on the other hand, argued, and continue to argue, that the famous clause was adopted as "shorthand" for the Bill of Rights, and that the framers utilized it both to broaden and to strengthen fundamental guarantees of rights and liberties. It is still possible to emerge with diverse conclusions, particularly in the light of the lengthy and heated congressional debates on the subject. Congressional "intent" is often as elusive as the Milky Way, and claims to it ought to be evaluated with considerable skepticism. What *is* certain is that since the Supreme Court first "incorporated" aspects of the Bill of Rights in 1925—arguably it was applied in one economic-proprietarian case in 1897—the process has been sporadic; but it proved to be increasingly embracing as well as continuous over the next four decades—although it may well have run its course now.

The earliest spokesman for total incorporation of the Bill of Rights was Justice John Marshall Harlan (1877-1911), the grandfather of the Justice John Marshall Harlan who served on the court from 1955 to 1971; but the elder Harlan was a lonely voice. In his thirty-four-year career on the highest bench, time and again he unsuccessfully championed that interpretation. He was not even partially vindicated until 1925 when Justice Edward T. Sanford delivered his famous dictum in *Gitlow v. New York*, stating that "we may and do assume that the First Amendment's free speech and press guarantees are enforceable against the states as well as against the national government."[6] Mr. Gitlow lost (and went to jail) but the "carry-over" principle had thus been judicially recognized. And as late as 1947 in the notable *Adamson* case, Justice Felix Frankfurter rejected the concept of incorporation as one manufactured out of whole cloth. Both the concept itself and the term "incorporation" were anathema to him. Indeed, his last publication before his death was an attack on "incorporation." As he put it in a well-known passage in the *Adamson* case:

Of all these [43] judges [of the Supreme Court who passed on the question of incorporating the Bill of Rights via the Due Process Clause of the Fourteenth Amendment] only one, *who may respectfully be called an eccentric exception*, ever indicated the belief that the Fourteenth Amendment was a shorthand summary of the first eight Amendments, therefore limiting only the Federal Government, and that due process incorporated those eight Amendments as restrictions upon the powers of the States.[7]

The "eccentric exception" was, of course, the elder Harlan—whose grandson, ironically, would be a Frankfurter ally on the incorporation question when he joined the Court as President Eisenhower's second appointee in 1955.

It was Justice Hugo L. Black who became the leading proponent of incorporation, and he seized upon the above-mentioned case of *Adamson v. California* to expound his views. At issue, briefly, was a provision of California law that permitted court and counsel to comment upon the failure of a defendant to explain or deny evidence against him, thus allowing the court and the jury to consider it in reaching a verdict. Admiral Dewey Adamson was under sentence of death for first degree burglary and and first degree murder, and had past convictions for burglary, larceny, and robbery. Adamson not only called no witnesses in his behalf but chose not to take the stand during his trial, a decision on which both the trial judge and the prosecuting attorney *commented adversely*. (Such comments have been statutorily proscribed on the *federal* level since 1878.) In his appeals, Adamson argued that the California law put him into an impossible situation: If he testified, the previous convictions would thus be revealed to the jury; and if he did not, comments by the judge and prosecutor would, in effect, convert his silence into a confession of guilt. (Only a few other states permitted the California procedure at the time.) In short, he claimed that the adverse comments by the two officials violated his constitutional privilege against compulsory self-incrimination under the Fifth Amendment of the federal Constitution, which he deemed incorporated and hence applicable to the states under the Due Process Clause of the Fourteenth. He ultimately *lost* five to four at the bar of the Supreme Court. In an opinion written by Justice Stanley F. Reed, and joined by Chief Justice Vinson and Associate Justices Robert H. Jackson and Harold H. Burton, the high tribunal held that the self-incrimination clause of the Fifth was *not* incorporated or applicable, and that the State of California "may control such a situation in accordance with its own ideas of the most efficient administration of criminal justice." Justice Frankfurter provided the decisive fifth vote in a characteristically long concurring opinion in which, as pointed out earlier, he took specific issue with the heart of Justice Black's dissenting opinion.

In his dissent, supported by a thirty-three-page appendix that quoted extensively from the congressional debates involving the Fourteenth Amendment, Black was joined wholly by Justice William O. Douglas and, in part, by Justices Frank Murphy and Wiley Rutledge (both of whom wanted to go even beyond Justice Black's position on incorporation—as indeed Douglas and others since ultimately would do). Justice Black's opinion remains the most celebrated analysis of the intention of the framers of Section 1. Elaborately researched, it insisted that one of the chief objects to be accomplished by the first section of the Fourteenth Amendment, "separately, and as a whole," was to apply the *entire* Bill of Rights to the states. In his own words:

My study of the historical events that culminated in the Fourteenth Amendment, and the expressions of those who opposed its submission and passage, persuades me that one of the chief objects that the provisions of the Amendment's first section, separately, and as a whole, were intended to accomplish was to make the Bill of Rights applicable to the states. With full knowledge of the *Barron* decision, the framers and backers of the Fourteenth Amendment proclaimed its purpose to be to overturn the constitutional rule that case had announced. This historical purpose had never received full consideration or expression in any opinion of this Court interpreting the Amendment....[8]

Responding to Justice Frankfurter's contrary view and call for more demonstrable proof (where Frankfurter believed none existed), Justice Black observed: "I cannot consider the Bill of Rights to be an outworn Eighteenth Century 'straight jacket.' ..." and concluded: "I believe [that] the original purpose of the Fourteenth Amendment [was] to extend to all the people of the nation the complete protection of the Bill of Rights. To hold that this Court can determine what, if any, provisions of the Bill of

Rights will be enforced, and if so to what degree, is to frustrate the great design of a written Constitution."[9]

Justice Black, in his almost three and a half decades on the Supreme Court, never wavered from these basic convictions—convictions buttressed by the expansive support extended to them by, among others, Professor W.W. Crosskey of the University of Chicago in a major essay a few years after *Adamson*. Black's staunchest historical-constitutional ally has been Professor Horace Flack. After a careful study of the debates of the Thirty-ninth Congress, their newspaper coverage, and the election speeches of members of Congress in the fall of 1866, Flack concluded that Congress "had the following objects and motives in view for submitting the First Section of the Fourteenth to the states for ratification. First, to make the National Bill of Rights applicable to the states; secondly, to give constitutional validity to the Civil Rights Act [of 1866]; and thirdly, to declare who were the citizens of the United States."[10]

But Black's opinion—though ardently supported by numerous constitutional scholars—was soon challenged in almost every detail by Professor Charles Fairman of the Harvard Law School, a leading expert on constitutional law, in an article in the *Stanford Law Review*. Fairman accused Black of deliberate distortion of the verities of the debates in the Thirty-ninth Congress to prove his point. In a companion article in the same issue, Professor Stanley Morrison, of the Stanford University School of Law, seconded Fairman's rejection of Black's thesis. But Morrison did so with considerably less vehemence, and not so much on the basis of what was said during the congressional debates as on the strength of the judicial history of the clause following the Amendment's adoption. Noting that only the elder Harlan had consistently supported Black's incorporation interpretation, Morrison sided with Frankfurter's analysis and statistics in his concurring opinion in the *Adamson* case. He refers to the refusal of such "libertarian activist" Justices as Holmes, Louis D. Brandeis,

Harlan F. Stone, Charles Evans Hughes [*sic*], and Benjamin Cardozo to incorporate the Bill of Rights and he *seems* to score a telling point by recalling that Black himself did not dissent from, or write a separate concurring opinion to, Cardozo's celebrated majority opinion in the 1937 case of *Palko v. Connecticut*.[11] That Cardozo opinion established a hierarchy of basic human rights which would henceforth be considered applicable to the states via the Fourteenth Amendment—namely, a *soi disant* "T" square that placed those "implicit in the concept of ordered liberty" on the one side—while at the same time establishing on the other side a *non-applicable* group, without which "justice would not perish." Among the former, comprising those rights and principles of justice "so rooted in the traditions and conscience of our people as to be ranked as fundamental," Cardozo cited speech, press, free exercise of religion, assembly, and petition of the First Amendment; due process of law of the Fifth Amendment and its eminent domain safeguards; right to counsel in criminal cases of the Sixth Amendment; and the overall concept of a "fair trial" in the Sixth, Seventh, and Eighth Amendments. Among the latter were all the other rights spelled out in Amendments One through Eight.

It is only fair to note at once here in Black's defense, however, that he had just joined the Court a few weeks earlier and thus he might well have believed that it would be ungracious as well as fool hardy to proclaim a new jurisprudential posture so early in his career. Further, the Cardozo majority opinion did, after all, announce the incorporation of the most precious of all basic human freedoms, notably First Amendment rights and, as Black himself had explained in his *Adamson* dissent, "[I]f the choice must be between the selective process of the *Palko* decision applying some of the Bill of Rights to the States, or the *Twining* rule (referring to an earlier decision) applying none of them, I would choose the *Palko* selective process." He reiterated in a footnote to his dissent in *Griswold v. Connecticut*[12] twenty-eight years after Palko, *that he "agreed to follow" the Palko* rule as a second-best method to "make [at least some of the] Bill of Rights safeguards applicable to the States." Although not as dramatically critical as Fairman, Morrison does suggest that Black clearly had an ulterior motive in his interpretation of the events surrounding the framing of the Fourteenth Amendment: The establishing of a rule of law for civil rights and liberties that would be both drastic and simple and that would guarantee certainly for all future litigation the carrying-over *in toto* of the Bill of Rights via the Fourteenth Amendment, through either its Due Process or its Privileges or Immunities Clauses.

A sixth protagonist, Professor J.B. James of Georgia Wesleyan College, in his 1956 book, *The Framing of the Fourteenth Amendment*,[13] agrees with Fairman and Morrison that Black's facile and sweeping interpretation of the congressional debates of 1866 is erroneous—but only *because* it is so sweeping and facile! With some reservations, James does share Black's and Flack's conclusion that, on balance, the Amendment's framers did intend to incorporate the Bill of Rights. Although such a thought may have been entirely foreign to the collective majority who supported its passage, James, as did Flack—and Professor Jacobus ten Broek, who shares most of James's views on the entire matter—presents strong evidence that the Amendment's *floor managers indeed intended its incorporation.* This is particularly true of Representative John A. Bingham, the author of the pertinent provisions of Section 1, whom Black called "without extravagance . . . the Madison [of that section] of the Fourteenth Amendment." Contrary to James's, and other earlier beliefs, we now know that, significantly, Bingham *was* fully aware of the Supreme Court's decision in *Barron v. Baltimore* when he led the debates on the Fourteenth Amendment in the House. As a matter of fact, it was this ruling, he said, which made necessary "the adopting of the [Fourteenth] Amendment." Certain in his belief that the Bill of Rights was designed to be *national* in scope, Bingham argued on the floor that had the Thirty-ninth congress meant the Bill of Rights to be solely applicable to the *federal* government, the wording of the Amendment's Section 1 would have so stated. James demonstrates quite convincingly that when Bingham and Republican Senator Jacob M. Howard of Michigan, the Amendment's floor manager in the upper house, spoke of the "fundamental rights of free men," they specifically meant the Bill of Rights. They wanted the proposed Amendment to overrule *Barron v. Baltimore!*

Senator Howard, in fact, clearly insisted that the national Bill of Rights *in its entirety* was incorporated into Section 1, a section that in his judgment embodied not only the "privileges and immunities" of Article Four, Paragraph 2, of the Constitution, but also all those rights guaranteed by the first eight amendments to the Constitution. Thus, in explaining the contents of the Amendment, he stated: "To these privileges and immunities [Art. Four, Par. 2], whatever they may be for they are not and cannot be fully defined . . . to these should be added the personal rights guaranteed and secured by the first eight amendments to the Constitution." Enumerating these, he continued: "[T]hese are secured to citizens solely as citizens of the United States, . . . they do not operate in the slightest degree as restraints or prohibitions upon state legislation. . . . *The great object of the first section of this amendment is, therefore, to restrain the power of the states and compel them at all times to respect these fundamental guarantees.*[14]

Nonetheless, Professor Fairman, with some support from Professor Morrison, still insists that the use of the phrases "fundamental rights" or "fundamental guarantees" was specifically intended to *exclude* the Bill of Rights. Fairman does admit that Senator Howard expressly stated that the Privileges or Immunities Clause of Section 1 of the Fourteenth should be construed as embracing what Howard termed "the personal rights" of the first eight amendments of the Bill of Rights. But Fairman insists that Bingham merely "talked around the point." Fairman's position received highly vocal support in 1977 with the publication of Professor Raoul Berger's fascinatingly controversial *Government by Judiciary: The Transformation of the Fourteenth Amendment.*[15] Berger concludes that his study of the "debates of the history of the period leads [him] fully to concur with Fairman," quoting approvingly Fairman's statement that the "freedom that states traditionally have exercised to develop their own systems of administering justice repels any thought that . . . Congress would . . . have attempted [to incorporate] . . . the country would not have stood for it, the legislatures would not have ratified."

The historians Alfred H. Kelly and Winfred A. Harbison, on the other hand, side with James's, Crosskey's, and Black's and his supporters' historical (and, incidentally, Black's constitutional) interpretation, and state flatly that Bingham and Howard not only agreed that the Privileges or Immunities Clause "incorporated the entire federal Bill of Rights as a limitation upon the states," but that the Due Process Clause was lifted from the Fifth Amendment and thus "became a guarantee against state action." And independent scholarly investigations by such knowledgeable legal commentators as Louis Henkin, Frank Walker, and Michael Curtis agree that there remains no genuine doubt that the framers of the Fourteenth Amendment intended it as a lever for the application of the Bill of Rights to the several states of the Union—with Curtis penning a learned point-by-point rebuttal of Raoul Berger's historical arguments. Curtis returned to the fray in a recent full-length book treatment of the issue, *No State Shall Abridge: The Fourteenth Amendment and the Bill of Rights*[16] strongly arguing the case for full incorporation. Although his evidence may be neither new nor definitive, Curtis demonstrates persuasively that, given the antislavery movement's role in the genesis of the Fourteenth Amendment, its framers did indeed appear to intend to apply the provisions of the entire Bill of Rights to the several states. Moreover, he offers an intriguing analysis of, and a convincing exhortation to resurrect, the long-emasculated Privileges or Immunities Clause of the Amendment's Section 1.

Regardless of personal intellectual and emotional commitments on the basic question of incorporation, the various
positions indicate how speculative history can be and may
become. The German historian Leopold von Ranke's exhortation
that it is essential to determine "*wie es eigentlich gewesen*" ("how it
actually was") is noble and human, but at times futile. However,
such evidence as the history of the debates provides appears to
substantiate Professor James's basic point that we need not
accept Justice Black's expansive evaluation of the events of the
Thirty-ninth Congress to side with his basic conclusion: there
seems little doubt that the Amendment's principal framers and
managers, Representative Bingham and Senator Howard, if not
every member of the majority in the two houses of Congress, did
believe the Bill of Rights to be made generally applicable to the
several states via Section 1, and they distinctly said so
consistently during the debates. And *no* member of that
Congress, before he voted on the Amendment, contradicted
Bingham's and Howard's final statements to that extent.

This conclusion does not, however, necessitate concurrence
with the matter of the *wisdom* of such an incorporation, nor with
the judicial formulae devised therefore. Nor does it gainsay the
fact that when Senator Howard's Privileges or Immunities
Clause (and his Representative Bingham's incorporation
contentions for it) had its first judicial test in the *Slaughter-
House Cases*[17] a mere five years after the adoption of the
Fourteenth Amendment, it sustained a crushing and lasting
defeat. Nor does the conclusion justify the two extremes of the
postures propounded by former Attorney General Edwin Meese,
on the one hand, namely that *no* incorporation whatsoever, was
intended by the history of phraseology of the Fourteenth
Amendment, and, on the other hand, that by Justice William J.
Brennan, namely, that the courts are to be encouraged, by virtue
of their quest for the attainment of justice, to use the Fourteenth
Amendment's language in whatever manner may be needed to
attain cherished perceived libertarian goals.

What is the current constitutional law of the Bill of Rights and its application or incorporation to the states? In short, Justice Black has triumphed—but not quite. Not quite because five of the enumerated rights in the Bill of Rights are still "out," i.e. not incorporated, yet they are relatively insignificant. Yet ironically and intriguingly, "not quite" also because the Court, led by Justice Douglas in the 1950s and 1960s, and since Douglas's departure notably by Justices Brennan and Marshall, has at least partially adopted the Murphy-Rutledge position in the *Adamson* case (a position that did not prevail then), namely: that if the verbiage of the Bill of Rights guarantees did not suffice to attain "justice" as they believed it to require, then the Court's resort to other, implied or inherent, provisions of the Constitution and even natural law, might be invoked. That policy of what Justice Black derided as "going upstairs," or by Justice Holmes as resorting to a "brooding omnipresence in the sky," was anathema to the great libertarian from Alabama, for he was a principled, devoted, consistent literalist. If it was not written down in the Constitution, it could not be utilized; but if it was spelled out—for example, the entire Bill of Rights' verbiage—Black viewed the literal commands of any provision as *absolutist*, especially the First Amendment's quintet of rights, which Justice Cardozo had pronounced as being "the matrix, the indispensable condition, of nearly every other form of freedom."

When Hugo Black joined the Court in 1937, only those rights subsequently listed in Justice Cardozo's "T" square of fundamental and non-fundamental rights as *fundamental* had been incorporated, or would soon be by virtue of Cardozo's 1937 *Palko* classification. Once he had planted his feet firmly on the highest bench in the land, Justice Black commenced on the odyssey that would become his lasting epitaph. Under *his* primary and superbly applied judicio—intellectual leadership, he would steer to triumphant incorporation, i.e. application to the fifty states—although frequently only by five-to-four or six-to-three votes—the following major Bill of Rights safeguards (all of which the states are thus now constitutionally bound to follow, in addition, of course, to those already applied earlier, notably all of the First Amendment's safeguards except the separation clause). Those that may be credited to Black's persuasiveness were:

1947 separation of Church and State (9 to 0)[18]
1948 public trial (7 to 2)
1961 "unreasonable"—but not "reasonable"—searches and
       seizures (6 to 3)
1962 cruel and unusual punishments (7 to 2)
1963 counsel in *all* criminal cases (9 to 0)
1964 self-incrimination (5 to 4)
1965 certain "unspecified" additional rights contained in the
       Ninth Amendment (7 to 2), with Black in predictable
       dissent here
1966 trial by an "impartial" jury (8 to 1)
1967 a "speedy" trail (9 to 0)
1968 trial by jury in all criminal cases (7 to 2)
1969 double jeopardy (6 to 2)

As the Supreme Court of the United States prepared to conclude its 1988-89 term in mid-1989—in the completion of its third term under Chief Justice Rehnquist, after seventeen under Chief Justice Warren Burger—no further provisions of the Bill of Rights had been incorporated since the double jeopardy clause in 1969. But, as indicated earlier, in effect only a few still remain "out," to wit: grand jury indictment; trial by a jury in *civil* cases; excessive bail and fines prohibitions; the so-called right to bear arms; and the Third Amendment's safeguards against involuntary quartering of troops in private homes. The close attention given during the sixteen years of the Warren Court's existence to problems of criminal justice, against the backdrop of fundamental concepts and concerns of due process of law, generally accepted as settled laws by successor courts, plus mounting legislative activity with such safeguards as bail, may well leave those few that are still "out," out. What is crucial is the increasing recognition and acceptance, both on and off the bench, that if there is anything at all "national" in scope and application under the United States Constitution, it is our fundamental civil rights and liberties.

It is this author's firm conviction that these cherished rights are assertively embraced and protected by the American judicial guardianship—a guardianship that is by no means confined to the Supreme Court of the United States at the apex of the judicial hierarchy—and, thus, are fundamentally secure. Indeed, the state courts have come around to an astonishingly gratifying degree, with a good many going well beyond the federal mandate in interpreting the Bill of Rights liberally. Thus, in some three hundred and fifty opinions since 1969, state courts have handed down decisions in civil rights and liberties litigation at a more advanced level than their federal counterparts. No wonder that the current U.S. Supreme Court's leading liberal activist, Justice Brennan, has counseled attorneys for libertarian causes to seek their successes in state courts, particularly in those at the apex of their judiciaries. That our basic rights are secure, notwithstanding sporadic crises, is a tribute to "We the People's" dedication to the finitely crucial principle that eternal vigilance is the price of liberty.

The Constitution is based on the hallowed imperative of majority rule with due regard for minority rights. Majority tyranny is barred, and so is minority tyranny. Hence, with an eye toward the towering and inconclusive Civil War days' struggle between President Abraham Lincoln and Chief Justice Robert B. Taney, and paraphrasing that wise jurist, Robert H. Jackson, it should be remembered that while excessively grandiose notions of majority rule are unacceptable, equally unacceptable are excessively grandiose notions of civil rights and liberties.

As Justice Jackson put it in dissent in a troubled case in 1949, *Terminiello v. Chicago*, while democratic society must be generous on the libertarian front, it is assuredly not obliged to be so doctrinaire and so devoid of practical wisdom as to "convert the constitutional Bill of Rights into a suicide pact."[19] The system, based upon the separation of powers, division of powers, and an intelligent, workable relationship or line between individual and societal rights and privileges, is a system with the irreducible aim of striving for those noble words atop the portals of the Supreme Court's magnificent edifice, "Equal Justice Under Law." It does *not* read "Equal Justice at Any Cost and Hang the Constitution." On all levels and in all seasons the government of the United States must always remain a government of laws, not a government of individuals. For laws are as the cement of society.

CHRONOLOGY OF THE BILL OF RIGHTS ERA[20]

26-28 September 1787	Debate by the Continental Congress over the failure to include a bill of rights in the Constitution.
November 1787	The Virginia House of Delegates calls for a state convention to meet in June to consider the proposed Constitution and possible amendments.
25 June 1788	Virginia ratifies the Constitution. Convention chooses a committee to report on proposed amendments to the Constitution.
27 June 1788	Virginia recommends a list of forty amendments to the Constitution.
8 November 1788	Virginia General Assembly elects Richard Henry Lee and William Grayson over James Madison to the Senate.
2 February 1789	George Washington elected president by the presidential electors.
30 April 1789	James Madison defeats James Monroe for a seat in Congress.
4 February 1789	George Washington inaugurated.
8 June 1789	Representative James Madison proposes constitutional amendments,

including a bill of rights, to be incorporated into the text of the Constitution.

14 July 1789	The Bastille falls in Paris.
24 August 1789	House of Representatives passes seventeen amendments.
27 August 1789	French National Assembly adopts *The Rights of Man, Citizen*.
9 September 1789	Senate passes twelve amendments.
24 September 1789	Congress establishes a Supreme Court, thirteen district courts, three circuit courts, and the position of attorney general.
25 September 1789	Both Houses approve twelve amendments to be sent to the states for ratification.
15 December 1791	Virginia is the eleventh and key state to ratify ten of the twelve amendments to the Constitution; the Bill of Rights becomes effective.

NOTES

1. Robert H. Jackson, *The Supreme Court in the American System of Government* (Cambridge: Harvard University Press, 1955), 23.
2. Robert Allen Rutland, *The Birth of the Bill of Rights,* rev. ed. (Boston: Northeastern University Press, 1983).
3. *Barron v. Baltimore,* 7 Peters 243 (1833).
4. Ibid. at 247-48, 250, 251.
5. Fourteenth Amendment, Section 1 (Ratified in 1868).

6. *Gitlow v. New York*, 268 U.S. 652 (1925) at 666.

7. *Adamson v. California*, 332 U.S. 46 (1947) at 62.

8. Ibid. at 71-72.

9. Ibid. at 89.

10. Horace Flack, *The Adoption of the Fourteenth Amendment* (Baltimore: Johns Hopkins University Press, 1908), 94.

11. *Palko v. Connecticut*, 302 U.S. 319 (1937).

12. *Griswold v. Connecticut*, 381 U.S. 479 (1965).

13. J.B. James, *The Framing of the Fourteenth Amendment* (Champaign, Ill.: University of Illinois Press, 1956).

14. *Congressional Globe*, Thirty-ninth Congress, 2765.

15. Raoul Berger, *Government by Judiciary: The Transformation of the Fourteenth Amendment* (Cambridge: Harvard University Press, 1977).

16. Michael Curtis, *No State Shall Abridge: The Fourteenth Amendment and the Bill of Rights* (Durham, N.C.: Duke University Press, 1986).

17. *Slaughter-House Cases*, 16 Wallace 36 (1873).

18. The vote on the merits at issue in the case was only five to four; but the Court was unanimous on the question of incorporation.

19. *Terminiello v. Chicago*, 337 U.S. 1 (1949) at 37.

20. Reproduced by permission of the *Virginia Independent*, 3 (October 1988): 4.

4

Original Intent and the Constitution Today

DOUGLAS LAYCOCK

Arguments about original intent are of two distinct kinds. One may argue over what the framers intended, and one may argue over the proper role of original intent in contemporary judicial decisions. What the framers intended is principally an argument about history—about the most accurate account of the past. The role of intent in judicial decisions is principally an argument about law—about theories of constitutional interpretation.

This distinction between the two arguments is real, but there is no strict separation between them. Hardly anyone believes that original intent is wholly irrelevant to constitutional interpretation. But unless one takes that position, the two arguments are inevitably interdependent. This does not arise merely from the psychological fact that everyone tends to give more weight to those views of the framers that they agree with, although that is an important source of interdependence.

More important, one's theory of constitutional interpretation may shape the inquiry into history. Each theory of constitutional interpretation emphasizes different historical questions. If one asks different questions, one will get different answers. If legal theorists conclude that some intentions are more important than others, or that some evidence of intent is more important than other evidence, this will change the legal conclusions that are drawn from history. That is why, as John Wilson has observed, lawyers and historians ask different questions about history.[1]

Similarly, one's inquiry into history may shape one's theory of constitutional interpretation. Some of the most important arguments against reliance on original intent in constitutional interpretation are that collective intent did not exist or cannot be known with sufficient accuracy, and that even if known, the intentions of 1789 are not responsive to the questions of 1989.[2] If a legal theory poses questions to history and historical inquiry determines that the questions are unanswerable, then the legal theory will have to be changed.

HOW TO LOOK FOR ORIGINAL INTENT

I find myself in the middle of both these debates. On the question of history, the original intent behind the religion clauses is more complex than either side wants to admit. If you find that the founders always agreed with you, you should probably reexamine your history.

On the question of constitutional theory, the intent of the founders matters, but it is not the only thing that matters, or even the most important. The most important source of constitutional meaning is the constitutional text. The people's representatives voted on the text. They did not vote on James Madison's notes, or the desultory debate in the House, or the secret debate in the Senate, or the private correspondence of the framers. They certainly did not vote on the constitutionality of everything the government did in the founding generation.

The ratified text has meaning to a language community that includes the present generation as well as the framers' generation. The text states sweeping principles. This nation has had two hundred years of experience in applying those principles to changing conditions, in arguing about them, in thinking about their implications. It is hardly surprising that the broad principles stated in the text turn out to have implications that the founders did not contemplate. So the search for intent is not for the founders' specific applications, and usually not for how the founders would have decided this case. Rather, the inquiry into original intent should proceed at the same level of generality as the text. If the framers had wanted a narrow list of specific rules with a detailed list of exceptions, they could have drafted that. They chose not to do so. They drafted broad principles that forbid whole categories of government misconduct in few words.

The search for intent must be for principles that are consistent with the text and as broad as the text, that solve the problems the founders addressed in their time, and that also give effect to constitutional values in the social conditions of our time. The inquiry into intent should ask what recent abuses the clause was directed to eliminate. What real controversies was the clause supposed to resolve? These are the problems they were thinking about when they drafted and ratified the clause, and these controversies can provide a center point to anchor the broader principle stated in the constitutional text.[3]

By contrast, much less weight should be ascribed to how the founders applied or failed to apply constitutional principles to cases that were not controversial in their time. Things that were not controversial received no serious scrutiny. They were not examined under the pressure of a real interest group with a real grievance. What the founders thought about is more important than what they did not think about. Not everything the founding generation did was constitutional even in their social conditions, and certainly not in ours.

The best evidence of their intent is found in real controversies, where one should not expect to find consensus. There were two sides to these controversies; there were winners and losers. Racism and discrimination did not instantly disappear when the Fourteenth Amendment was ratified, and one should not expect religious intolerance or support for establishment to instantly disappear when the First Amendment was ratified.

Finally, little can be learned from the legislative history as such—from the records of debates and the founders' explanations of what they meant. Most of that material was not recorded. Much of what was recorded was recorded inaccurately; shorthand was in its infancy. Both contemporary complaints and modern scholarship attest to these points.[4] Even if the legislative history is accepted at face value, it is remarkably unrevealing. The inferences one can draw from it are generally attenuated, lacking power to persuade. Some of the clearest statements seem inconsistent with large bodies of other evidence. This essay reviews what survives on the religion clauses. But it is more fruitful to examine the social, intellectual, and political history of the founding generation, and the great controversies of their time.

ORIGINAL INTENT ABOUT DISESTABLISHMENT

CONFLICTING EVIDENCE AND ATTEMPTS TO RECONCILE IT

The founders' treatment of religious liberty does not easily fit into the modern conceptions of any faction. By emphasizing different parts of the historical record, different scholars and justices have created dramatically inconsistent accounts of original intent. Few of these accounts have dealt effectively, or at all, with the evidence that supports other accounts.

Beginning with *Everson v. Board of Education*,[5] the Supreme Court's official history was a strict separationist history. The Court emphasized the history of religious persecution, the fight for disestablishment, the views of James Madison and Thomas Jefferson, and the Virginia Statute for Religious Liberty. The Court concluded that government must be neutral toward religion, and not support it in any way.

The Court's critics,[6] and some of the Court's recent opinions,[7] emphasize very different aspects of history. Government in the founders' generation constantly supported religion. Congress appointed chaplains who offered daily prayers. Presidents proclaimed days of prayer and fasting. The government paid for missionaries to the Indians. The Northwest Ordinance set aside land to endow schools because, the statute recited, "religion, morality, and knowledge" are necessary to good government.[8] That provision was a compromise,[9] but the compromise implied that Congress expected that the schools thus endowed would teach religion. Events confirmed the expectation. Some states retained established churches, and most enforced Sabbath laws and blasphemy laws. Most of the states that enforced such laws had their own constitutional guarantees of religious liberty. Even Madison and Jefferson supported some of these measures.

Neither side relies on other practices of the founders' generation. No one relies on their widespread anti-Catholicism[10] or the test oaths that barred Catholics from holding office or even voting in several states.[11] But those are also part of the historical record.

The challenge for anyone trying to make sense of original intent is to account for all this evidence in a principled way. Is there a pattern to the founders' treatment of church and state? Is there an implicit principle on which they acted? Or is there simply an ad hoc series of inconsistent actions? The *Everson* account ignores these problems; it follows Madison on his good days and ignores the rest.

The Court's critics have tried to account for more of the evidence. Their most common claim is that the founders intended to permit government aid to religion so long as that aid does not prefer one religion over others. This non-preferentialist thesis has been around for a long time, and the Supreme Court has repeatedly rejected it.[12] But it has refused to die. In this decade, it has been offered by former Attorney General Edwin Meese,[13] Chief Justice William H. Rehnquist,[14] political scientists Michael Malbin[15] and Robert Cord,[16] law professor Rodney Smith, [17] and the United States Catholic Conference.[18]

A recent article by law professor Steven Smith offers a different theory.[19] He concludes that the founders intended the strict institutional separation of church and state. By that he means that the state should not exercise ecclesiastical power or interfere with the internal affairs of churches, and that the churches as such should not exercise government power or interfere in the internal affairs of government. But he concludes that that is all the founders intended. He believes the founders did not intend—indeed, could not imagine—a secular state separated from religious belief and observance.

None of these theories fit the historical data. The Supreme Court's simple account in *Everson* ignores too much data without justification. One has to try to understand how the founders' seeming inconsistencies fit together in their time before rejecting any part of what they did. Neither side can just pick the parts it likes or assume that the whole nation agreed with Madison.

The nonpreferentialist account flies in the face of the data. Nonpreferentialism is one of the few issues the founders clearly considered and decided. Nonpreferentialism was the last compromise offered by the defenders of establishment, and the founding generation repeatedly rejected it.

Institutional separation was surely an important part of what the founders sought to accomplish, but their fights for disestablishment went beyond that. The opponents of establishment opposed all forms of financial aid to churches, including aid that

would be delivered in ways arguably consistent with institutional separation. But a more fundamental disagreement with
Steven Smith is over an issue of constitutional theory: the significance of the founders' failure to think about an issue.

This essay will fill in the historical information to support
these conclusions about nonpreferentialism and institutional
separation, and then suggests a different set of principles to
account for the evidence of the founders' intent.

THE FIGHT OVER DISESTABLISHMENT IN THE STATES

The American Revolution provoked a general rethinking of
church-state relations in many of the new states. Most of the
states wrote constitutions, and where there was disagreement
about church-state relations, the process of constitution writing
focused attention on it. In the states with established Anglican
churches, George III was head of the church as well as head of
the state. The Revolution posed a question of succession in both
capacities. The Virginia legislature's first reaction was to direct
that wherever the Book of Common Prayer said to pray for the
King, the people should pray for the legislature.[20] At the cost of
considerable simplification, there emerged three main patterns:
the southern colonies, the middle colonies, and New England.

Virginia and the Other Southern Colonies. Virginia is the best
exemplar of the Southern colonies. In 1776, the Virginia Declaration of Rights guaranteed the free exercise of religion.[21] Also in
1776, Virginia suspended collection of the tax to support the
Anglican clergy. But the statute recited that the legislature had
made no decision concerning a more general tax to support all
clergy.[22] That issue was reserved for the future, and it was
debated intermittently for ten years.

In 1784 a general assessment bill passed two readings in the
legislature. The bill assessed a tax to support teachers of the
Christian religion.[23] But it provided that each citizen could
designate the pastor to get his tax. Any Christian teacher was

eligible—even Catholic priests. Taxpayers could even designate a fund for schools, so that non-Christians were provided for without being expressly mentioned. There was an exemption for Quakers and Mennonites, who had no paid clergy and conscientiously objected to such a tax. In short, the bill was as nonpreferential as Americans in the 1780s could imagine.

Madison got the final vote delayed to the next session so that legislators could consult their constituents. The bill was then defeated by a broad coalition, including the usual number of votes opposed to any tax. Madison was a part of that coalition, but he was only a part, and probably is given too much credit.[24] It was in this context that he wrote his "Memorial and Remonstrance Against Religious Establishments," perhaps the classic short statement of the arguments for disestablishment.[25]

Religious denominations also played a critical role. The Baptists were the most vigorously opposed. Baptists believed that they should support their church voluntarily; they were conscientiously opposed to having that support coerced by the state.

The Methodists were also opposed. They were a smaller group, just then breaking off from the Anglicans. Whether out of principle, or just to distinguish themselves from the Anglicans, they were opposed.

The Presbyterians were a large minority, and they initially supported the bill. A tax for churches looked more attractive if they would benefit. But when Hanover Presbytery met and fully considered the issue, it came out opposed. Their opposition was based at least in part on self-interest. Presbyterian polity carefully balances power between clergy and laity. Part of the laity's control is financial: a church contracts with a minister and sets his salary. If the clergy were supported by a tax collected by the state, in an amount set by statute, the laity would lose that financial check, and the balance of power would be upset.

The Presbyterians were the last straw. When they joined the coalition against the bill, the bill was dead. Indeed, it never came to a vote.

The lessons most commonly drawn from this debate are that Virginians rejected an established church, which is true, and that they agreed on everything in the "Memorial and Remonstrance," which is probably not true.

Two other lessons are more important. First, the issue was nonpreferentialism. The bill was as nonpreferential as its supporters could make it, and the issue was precisely whether that feature made it acceptable. The answer was no.

Second, nonpreferentialism was impossible to implement even then in a state where the religious faiths were almost entirely Protestant and where religious diversity ran only from Anglicans to Baptists. Despite the efforts of leading Virginians and Virginia's relative homogeneity, it was impossible to implement the general assessment in a way that was acceptable to all denominations. The bill would have violated the consciences of the Baptists and upset the polity of the Presbyterians. If nonpreferentialism was impossible then, it is hard to see how it would work now, in a vastly more pluralistic society.

In 1786, in the wake of this debate, the legislature enacted Jefferson's Statute for Religious Liberty, with its provision that no person shall be compelled to frequent or support any place of worship whatsoever.[26] That language is broad enough to forbid both preferential and nonpreferential support for churches.

The other southern colonies followed somewhat similar paths with much less debate. Maryland defeated a similar bill in 1785 after a statewide debate.[27] Georgia enacted such a bill but never collected the tax; it was repealed by the constitution of 1798.[28] North Carolina disestablished without a significant fight.[29] South Carolina retained a vestigial establishment of Protestantism into the national period; proposals for a nonpreferential tax briefly surfaced and went nowhere.[30]

The Middle Colonies (and Rhode Island). In the middle colonies, there is not much to report. There was no establishment in Pennsylvania, Delaware, or New Jersey, or in Rhode Island, a New England colony that was like a middle colony for this purpose.[31] The vestigial establishment in New York faded away without much debate.[32]

Massachusetts and the Rest of New England. The other great pattern was that of New England, and the examplar was Massachusetts.[33] The Massachusetts constitution of 1780 enacted a local option establishment. There was a tax to support the minister established by law, to be selected by local vote and settled by contract in each parish. In theory any denomination could win the election. Dissenters could file exemption certificates and pay the tax to their own church instead.

The convergence with the Virginia proposals is remarkable. The strategy was nonpreferential. John Adams said that Massachusetts had "the most mild and equitable establishment of religion that was known in the world, if indeed, it could be called an establishment."[34]

Dissenters did not find it so mild and equitable; the system was not so nonpreferential in practice. The Congregationalists won nearly all the local elections, and that was understood and intended. The Baptists and Quakers refused on grounds of conscience to file for exemption certificates—Quakers because they had no paid clergy and Baptists because they would support their clergy only with voluntary contributions. The authorities regularly levied on their property for unpaid taxes, which of course went to support the Congregationalists. Other dissenters sometimes had trouble qualifying for exemptions, either because of unsympathetic administration of the law or because their church was not incorporated.[35]

This establishment persisted until the Congregationalists began to lose elections to the Unitarians. Then the establishment looked onerous indeed. The last remnants of formal establishment were repealed in 1833.

Connecticut had a very similar system, with the same problems.[36] New Hampshire and Vermont had systems that were quite similar in theory, but in practice they were less organized and there was more local diversity.[37]

Conclusions from the Debates in the States. Several conclusions may be drawn from this survey of the debates of the 1780s. First, some version of nonpreferentialism was on the agenda in every state where the debate got serious.

Second, the debates in Virginia were the fullest development of this widespread argument. That is what makes Virginia so important. It is not just that some of us like the Virginia outcome, or even that Madison and Jefferson were there. It is that the Virginians most fully developed the arguments that were going on all up and down the country.

Third, the remnants of establishment in New England did not work. They caused bitter religious strife and were repealed early in the national period. They were remnants of the old regime, not models for the new. The nonpreferentialists simply cannot account for this widespread rejection of their theory.

This author does not think that Steven Smith can fully account for it either, although that is a closer case. In Virginia and Maryland, there was no clear issue of institutional separation. The issue was financial aid to churches, delivered in a way that minimized contact between church and state. The state would not interfere with the internal affairs of the churches; it would simply turn over the money to the church designated by the taxpayer.

The distinction between financial aid and institutional interference was part of the debate of 1784-85. Hanover Presbytery drew the distinction explicitly. In the fall of 1784, the Presbytery passed a resolution supporting a general assessment on condition that the state recognize full equality of religious bodies and full freedom for all faiths, and that there be no interference with creeds, forms of worship, and internal church affairs.[38] The state could provide tax support so long as it kept its hands off internal church affairs.

The Presbyterians eventually changed their mind, in part because they concluded that the issues could not be so cleanly separated. Tax support upset internal affairs in some churches, most notably in the disruption of Presbyterian polity. And perhaps Smith would say that letting the state perform the church function of collecting contributions is itself a violation of institutional separation. But it seems clear that much of the opposition was to the principle of government support for the churches, and not just to institutional combination. In Madison's words, the extraction of three pence was an establishment.[39]

THE LEGISLATIVE HISTORY

The Rejected Drafts. As noted earlier, the legislative history is often unhelpful. But in this case, the legislative history offers a remarkable confirmation of the rejection of nonpreferentialism. The Senate and the Conference Committee appear to have squarely considered the choice between forbidding any establishment or forbidding only nonpreferential establishments.[40] The Senate met in secret and did not record its debates, but it recorded motions and votes in a journal. The Senate considered four drafts of the Establishment Clause that unambiguously stated the nonpreferentialist theory:

Congress shall make no law establishing one religious sect or society in preference to others. . . .

Congress shall not make any law . . . establishing any Religious Sect or Society.

Congress shall make no law establishing any particular denomination of religion in preference to another. . . .

Congress shall make no law establishing articles of faith or a mode of worship. . . .

The first three of these drafts were rejected in the Senate. A week later, the Senate adopted the draft limited to "articles of faith or a mode of worship." That draft was rejected in the Conference Committee.

The Conference Committee produced the version ultimately ratified: "Congress shall make no law respecting an establishment of religion. . . ." This is one of the broadest drafts considered by either House. It forbids any law respecting an establishment of "religion." It does not say "a religion," "a national religion," "a single religion," "a particular religion," "one sect or society," or "any particular denomination of religion." It is religion generically that may not be established.

This drafting history is not quite as dispositive as it would be in the case of a statute. The assent of state legislatures was required to amend the Constitution, and one may not assume without evidence that state legislatures were familiar with the rejected Senate drafts. But the rejected drafts are important for several reasons. First, the rejection of nonpreferentialism in the First Congress is consistent with all the other rejections of nonpreferentialism in the founding generation. Second, the Virginia, New York, and North Carolina ratifying conventions had proposed nonpreferentialist amendments similar to the rejected Senate drafts, and those proposals had circulated around the country.[41] So even if state legislatures could not compare the actual amendment to the rejected Senate drafts, they could compare it to earlier state proposals and see the difference.

Third, although Congress could not unilaterally amend the Constitution, it could unilaterally prevent amendments by any procedure other than a new convention. So the Congressional rejection of nonpreferential drafts was dispositive, even though the Congressional proposal of the actual clause was only a proposal. It is accurate to say that the First Congress considered and authoritatively rejected proposals to forbid only preferential establishments. The persistence of nonpreferentialism in the face of this rejection is extraordinary.

The Legislative Debates. The legislative debates say little. They do not support any of the theories under consideration, but they do provide one startling piece of evidence for an interpretation even narrower than nonpreferentialism. The only recorded debate on the religion clauses occurred in the House of Representatives on 15 August 1789.[42] The reporter's notes fill slightly less than two columns in the *Annals of Congress*. The debate concerned the draft submitted by a Select Committee, and a substitute offered by Samuel Livermore. Both drafts were somewhat different from the amendment ultimately adopted. The Select Committee draft provided: "No religion shall be established by law, nor shall the equal rights of conscience be infringed." The Livermore substitute provided: "Congress shall make no laws touching religion, or infringing the rights of conscience."

Fifty-one representatives were present to vote on the Livermore amendment. Only eight of them said anything the reporter took down, and five of the eight said things that cast no light on meaning. Someone suggested transposing the order of the two clauses; another said no bill of rights was needed; another agreed but said it would do no harm and reassure doubters, and so on. They may have been an assembly of demigods, but their minutes sound like any other committee meeting.

Two speakers—Peter Sylvester and Benjamin Huntington —opposed the Establishment Clause. Some nonpreferentialists seem to think they were authoritatively describing the clause.[43] Instead, they were urging its deletion or at least a minimalist interpretation. One of them offered to explain "the blessed fruits" of disestablishment in Rhode Island, another sarcastic reference of the kind Edwin S. Gaustad has described earlier in this volume.[44] The speaker did not mean that disestablishment would provide blessed fruits if it were narrowly conceived.

The heart of the argument is Madison. Madison chose not to argue with Sylvester and Huntington, but to reassure them and their sympathizers by portraying the Establishment Clause in the narrowest possible light. He spoke twice, and both remarks are a puzzle. First he said: "He apprehended the meaning of the words to be, that Congress should not establish a religion, and enforce the legal observation of it by law, nor compel men to worship God in any manner contrary to their conscience."[45]

Later, he proposed that the House insert the word "national" before the word "religion," so that the Establishment Clause would read: "No national religion shall be established by law." Madison explained that "he believed that the people feared one sect might obtain a pre-eminence, or two combine together, and establish a religion to which they would compel others to conform. He thought that if the word "national" was introduced, it would point the amendment directly to the object it was intended to prevent."[46]

What did he mean by that? His proposed amendment, "no national religion," is consistent with nonpreferentialism. His explanation is much narrower. If Congress appropriated one million dollars for the support of the United Methodist Church, it would not be enforcing the observation of Methodism by law. Yet the appropriation would be preferential, unconstitutional even under the nonpreferentialist interpretation of the Clause. Whatever Madison described, it was not nonpreferentialism. Neither did he describe an amendment focused on institutional separation. To his credit, Steven Smith does not rely on these remarks.

It is hard to know what Madison was thinking. The two statements are inconsistent with all his previous and subsequent statements concerning establishment. Nevertheless, he appears to have said the same thing clearly and twice. Maybe the reporter garbled it both times, but it seems likely that Madison said something approximating what the reporter attributes to him. The two statements are also consistent with Madison's 8 June draft of the Clause, which provided only that no "national religion be established."

This writer's best guess is that on 8 June and 15 August, this was all Madison thought he could get, but that by the time of the Conference Committee, he saw a chance to get more. Passage was not assured on 15 August; Madison had spent the whole session just getting the amendments to the floor of the House. Many Federalists thought amendments were unnecessary; Anti-Federalists foresaw that passing amendments would take away their best criticism of the new Constitution. Congress was occupied with more urgent matters like organizing the other two branches and raising the revenue to run them.

If Madison had been describing the final draft, his remarks would be more important, but he was not. His proposal to insert the word "national" provoked a collateral attack by Elbridge Gerry. Gerry said that the Anti-Federalists had always known this was a national government and not a federal government, and here was Madison confirming the charge by using the word "national." Madison withdrew his suggestion. He could have substituted a less offensive word: "single," "particular," or "specific" would have done nicely; even "federal" might have worked. He offered none of these, and no more was heard of the "no national religion" language. It is not the Establishment Clause; it is yet another rejected draft.

At this point someone called the question on Livermore's substitute, and it was adopted. The only reported debate thus ended a lot further from the no-preference position than it began. Livermore's substitute was inelegant but sweeping. It forbad any law "touching" religion, which would include both preferential and nonpreferential laws, any form of aid or interference. No one in this brief debate said that preferential establishments were bad while nonpreferential ones were acceptable. Only three people spoke to the merits; two of them appear to have been in the minority; and no one on any side accepted Madison's explanation.

In the month that followed, explicitly nonpreferential drafts were fought over and rejected in the Senate and the Conference Committee. The debates were not recorded, but the choices were clearly presented. Whatever the founders meant, it was not that preferential establishments are forbidden but non-preferential establishments are allowed.

THE FOUNDERS' OTHER INTENT: CIVIL RELIGION

Non-financial Aid. Government in the founding generation actively supported religious belief in a variety of ways that required no transfer of funds from government to churches. What is one to make of the Congressional chaplains, the days of prayer and fasting, the Sabbath laws, the Northwest Ordinance, and all the rest? Is there some principle that reconciles these practices with the views expressed in the debates over disestablishment?

It is significant that the founders saw no problem with government sponsorship and endorsement of generic Protestantism. They saw no problem with it because in their society, no one complained. It did no apparent harm, no one raised the issue, and they had no occasion to seriously think about it. Just as the framers excluded blacks from the proposition that all men are created equal, they less consciously, less pervasively, and less cruelly excluded non-Protestants from the proposition that government should not establish religion. If a practice was not controversial among Protestants, it was not controversial at all. Government support for generic Protestantism is not evidence of what the Establishment Clause means, because the founders were not seriously thinking about the Establishment Clause when they did these things.

The heart of my disagreement with Steven Smith is the question of what inference to draw from things the founders failed to think about. I say that they did not seriously think about it, and so they had no intent for us to follow, and we must apply for ourselves the principle stated in the constitutional text. He says that they did not think about it, and so they did not intend to forbid it, and therefore it is not forbidden. To put his point another way, he would say that we are bound by the consensus that caused them not to think about it.

This writer's disagreement with Smith is not so much over history as over the theory of constitutional interpretation. I would *enforce* the broad principle ratified in the text, *in light of* the principal controversies that appear to have led to it. Smith would *narrow* the broad principle ratified in the text, to cover *only* the principal controversies that appear to have led to it. Both the bare text and the principles reflected in the founders' debate over disestablishment have implications for government endorsements of generic Christianity in a nation with millions of non-Christians. One may not ignore those implications just because the social conditions of the founders' time failed to focus attention on them. The municipal creche is divisive today just as the general assessment was divisive then, and both are forms of government support for religion. Those of us who would forbid the creche are taking the principles the founders developed in the context of division between Anglicans and Baptists, and applying them to today's divisions between Christians, Jews, Muslims, Buddhists, agnostics, and atheists.

Missionaries to the Indians. One of the founders' practices requires separate consideration. For a century, the government paid missionaries to educate the Indians.[47] In some cases, the government sent missionaries in exchange for Indian lands. These programs cannot be characterized as non-financial; money was paid out to churches. Yet it was somehow considered a different category from things like the general assessment. Madison and Jefferson participated, and no one seriously objected.

The most obvious explanation is that the government was buying secular services from churches, or paying churches to perform governmental tasks. This has profound implications for aid to parochial schools and for church delivery of social services. It is possible that the founders did not think of the missionaries in these terms. Perhaps they placed these programs in a separate category for Indians, considered as foreign sovereigns, wards of the government, or some combination of the two. That proposition is hard to test, because the federal government did not deliver social services to white citizens. States did only a little more. It would be useful to know whether churches and local governments cooperated financially for the relief of the poor. When Virginia disestablished the Anglican church, the state took over poor relief from the church.[48] I do not know whether this reflected a conscious decision about disestablishment, or was simply a consequence of cutting off the church's tax revenue.

Like civil religion, the founders do not appear to have thought much about missionaries to the Indians. It was not a subject of serious controversy. Support for missionaries cannot be attributed simply to the founders' Protestant bias, because the government occasionally paid for Catholic missionaries, too. Maybe it was a product of Christian bias. Maybe it was just a good way to get the job done.

To conclude that the founders did not think about this much largely eliminates their intent as a factor. Apparently, they did not consciously intend for the Establishment Clause to permit such church-state cooperation. But even more obviously, they did not consciously intend for the Establishment Clause to forbid it. One cannot argue against aid to parochial schools on the basis of any direct evidence of the founders' intent.

The question in modern times is to identify those government services that establish religion if given, and those that must be given to avoid discriminating against religion. In *Everson v. Board of Education*, the Court was nine to zero on the principle that government should not aid religion, but it was five to four on whether bus rides to transport children to school constituted aid. Those two divisions reflect the relative difficulty of the questions. The general assessment bill, with special taxes earmarked for the support of clergy, was clearly aid. Bus rides and many other things in the modern social welfare state are not so clear. This is a case where the answers of 1789 are not responsive to the questions of 1989.

A BRIEF NOTE ON FREE EXERCISE

There is less to say about the Free Exercise Clause. Its intellectual and legislative history has been less accessible, and it has received vastly less attention from judges and scholars. The controversies about free exercise in the founder's time received less attention than the controversies over establishment, and the Free Exercise Clause received much less debate. But there is more evidence of original intent than scholars have realized. Michael McConnell has just completed the first thorough marshalling of the evidence.[49]

There was of course a great formative controversy in the founders' collective memory, relevant both to free exercise and to establishment. This was the history of religious persecution and religious warfare in the wake of the Reformation. The memory of serious religious conflict was more recent to the founders than the memory of slavery is to us, and minor persecutions continued into their political lifetimes.[50] It is surely reasonable to infer that the founders intended the religion clauses to prevent such conflicts here.

One lesson of religious persecutions is that some humans will die for their faith, and others will kill for it. The religion clauses are designed in part to protect these unusually fervent believers, and to protect others from them. Religious minorities need not be reasonable; the religion clauses exist in part because religious minorities are not reasonable.

Another lesson of religious persecutions is that the Free Exercise Clause must protect religiously motivated conduct, as well as belief and speech. Conscientious objectors to government policy are willing to suffer greatly rather than violate their conscience; attempts to coerce religious conscience lead inevitably to persecution.[51]

McConnell identifies three significant controversies over exemptions for conscientious objection in the founding period: over oath-taking, over military conscription, and over payment of religious taxes.[52] In each of these cases, legislatures granted exemptions, and the prevailing understanding was that the legislature would violate religious liberty if it refused such exemptions. This understanding informs the meaning of the judicially enforceable guarantees of free exercise that appeared in state constitutions and in the First Amendment.

That inference is in turn confirmed by the frequent provisos in state constitutions, restricting religious exercise to acts that did not breach the peace or threaten the peace and safety of the state.[53] These provisos limit freedom of religious conduct; no one would have thought them necessary if free exercise clauses protected only religious belief. They tend to confirm that free "exercise" means what it says—that it includes conduct as well as belief.

A wholly uninformed Supreme Court has taken a different view. In an opinion with staggering implications, the Supreme Court has held that the free exercise clause does not protect religious conduct from facially neutral laws.[54] The Court held that criminal punishment of Native American worship services raised no issue under the Free Exercise Clause and required no government justification whatever! It was enough that the worship service used peyote and that the use of peyote was forbidden by a law that made no reference to religion. The same reasoning could be applied to communion wine in a dry jurisdiction, to ordination of women and homosexuals, to Sabbatarians seeking accommodations made necessary by the Christian calender, and to a host of other issues. At a stroke, the Court reduced the Free Exercise Clause to a redundant appendage of the Free Speech and Equal Protection Clauses.

The question was neither raised nor briefed by anyone. The majority consisted mostly of justices who claim to follow original intent, but they appeared totally unaware that there was any evidence of intent on this issue. The result is that religious minorities will suffer for conscience in America, and the federal courts are closed to them.

CONCLUSION

Occasionally the founders' intent is clear and applicable, as in their conclusion that nonpreferential establishments were still establishments and still objectionable. More often, their intent is unclear, or not responsive to the questions asked in our time. Sometimes, their intent is a starting point for a line of reasoning that must be completed. Thus, when one concludes that conscientious objectors must be protected to avoid religious persecution, we start with the founders' intention to avoid persecution, but fill in most of the rest of the argument ourselves.

We cannot escape the responsibility of self-government; we must decide for ourselves how to apply the Constitution in our time. But if self-government is to consist mostly of majority rule, and only sometimes of judicial interpretation, then constitutional interpretation must start with the text of the Constitution, and with such clear and applicable evidence of intent as can be found.

NOTES

1. John F. Wilson, "Original Intent and the Quest for Comparable Consensus," pp. 113-33.
2. See, e.g., Paul Brest, "The Misconceived Quest for the Original Understanding," *Boston University Law Review* 60 (1980):204.
3. These points are further developed in Douglas Laycock, "Text, Intent, and the Religion Clauses," *Notre Dame Journal of Law, Ethics & Public Policy* 4 (1989):93.

4. See James H. Hutson, "The Creation of the Constitution: The Integrity of the Documentary Record," *Texas Law Review* 65 (1986):1,6; Marion Tinling, "Thomas Lloyd's Reports of the First Federal Congress," *William & Mary Quarterly*, 3d ser., 18 (1961):519.

5. *Everson v. Board of Education*, 330 U.S. 1 (1947).

6. The most thorough of this work is Robert L. Cord, *Separation of Church and State: Historical Fact and Current Fiction* (New York: Lambeth Press, 1982). See also *Wallace v. Jaffree*, 472 U.S. 38 (1985) at 91-114 (Rehnquist, J., dissenting).

7. *Lynch v. Donnelly*, 465 U.S. 668 (1984); *Marsh v. Chambers*, 463 U.S. 783 (1983).

8. The Northwest Ordinance is reprinted in a footnote to Act of Aug. 7, 1789, ch. 8, 1 Stat. 50.

9. Edwin S. Gaustad, "Religion and Ratification," pp. 41-59.

10. See Douglas Laycock, "'Nonpreferential' Aid to Religion: A False Claim About Original Intent," *William & Mary Law Review* 27 (1986):875, 918.

11. Gaustad, "Religion and Ratification," pp. 41-59.

12. *Wallace v. Jaffree* at 52-55; *Abington School District v. Schempp*, 374 U.S. 203 (1963) at 216-17; *Illinois ex rel. McCollum v. Board of Education*, 333 U.S. 203 (1948) at 211.

13. Edwin Meese, III, "The Supreme Court of the United States: Bulwark of a Limited Constitution," *South Texas Law Journal* 27 (1986):455, 464.

14. *Wallace v. Jaffree*, at 91-114 (Rehnquist, J., dissenting).

15. Michael J. Malbin, *Religion and Politics: The Intentions of the Authors of the First Amendment* (Washington, D.C.: American Enterprise Institute for Public Policy Research, 1978).

16. Cord, *Separation of Church and State*.

17. Rodney K. Smith, "Getting Off on the Wrong Foot and Back on Again: A Reexamination of the History of the Framing of the Religion Clauses of the First Amendment and a Critique of the *Reynolds* and *Everson* Decisions," *Wake Forest Law Review* 20 (1984):569.

18. Brief of the United States Catholic Conference as Amicus Curiae in Support of Appellants 10-15, in *Aguilar v. Felton* (No. 84-237), 473 U.S. 402 (1985).

19. Steven D. Smith, "Separation and the 'Secular': Reconstructing the Disestablishment Doctrine," *Texas Law Review* 67 (1989):955.

20. Thomas E. Buckley, *Church and State in Revolutionary Virginia, 1776-1787* (Charlottesville: University Press of Virginia, 1977), 21.

21. 9 Hening's Statutes at Large 109, 111-12 par. 16 (1821). The clause is quoted in Thomas J. Curry, *The First Freedoms: Church and State in America to the Passage of the First Amendment* (New York: Oxford University Press, 1986), 146.

22. This statute is reprinted in Buckley, *Church and State*, 35 and in Anson P. Stokes, *Church and State in the United States*, 3 vols. (New York: Harper & Brothers, 1950), 1:305.

23. The bill is reprinted in *Everson* at 72-74 (appendix to opinion of Rutledge, J., dissenting), in Buckley, *Church and State*, 188-89, and in Cord, *Separation of Church and State*, 242-43.

24. For more detailed accounts, see Buckley, *Church and State*, 113-43; Curry, *First Freedoms*, 140-48; William L. Miller, *The First Liberty: Religion and the American Republic* (New York: Knopf, 1985), 24-36.

25. The "Memorial and Remonstrance" is reprinted in *Everson* at 63-72 (appendix to opinion of Rutledge, J., dissenting); Cord, *Separation of Church and State*, 244-49; Saul K. Padover, ed., *The Complete Madison: His Basic Writings* (New York: Harper, 1953), 299-306.

26. The statute is still in effect. Va. Code Ann. 57-1 (1986). It is reprinted in Buckley, *Church and State*, 190-91; Cord, *Separation of Church and State*, 249-50; and Stokes, *Church and State*, 1:392-94.

27. Curry, *First Freedoms*, 155-57; Forrest McDonald, *Novus Ordo Seclorum: The Intellectual Origins of the Constitution* (Lawrence, Kan.: University Press of Kansas, 1985), 43-44.

28. Curry, *First Freedoms*, 152-53; Stokes, *Church and State*, 1:440.

29. Curry, *First Freedoms*, 151.

30. Ibid., 149-51. The South Carolina statute is reprinted in Stokes, *Church and State*, 1:432-34.

31. Curry, *First Freedoms*, 159-60, 162.

32. Ibid., 161-62.

33. For a review of the New England experience see ibid., 162-92; William G. McLoughlin, *New England Dissent 1630-1833: The Baptists and the Separation of Church and State* (Cambridge, Mass.: Harvard University Press, 1971). For more on Massachusetts only, see Jacob C. Meyer, *Church and State in Massachusetts from 1740 to 1833: A Chapter in the History of the Development of Individual Freedom* (Cleveland: Western Reserve University, 1930).

34. Curry, *First Freedoms*, 131.

35. See *Barnes v. First Parish*, 6 Mass. 400 (1810) (holding that minister

of unincorporated religious society was not entitled to church taxes paid by his adherents). Incorporation in those days required a special act of the legislature; general incorporation laws were not enacted until much later.

36. Curry, *First Freedoms*, 178-84.

37. Ibid., 184-90.

38. Miller, *First Liberty*, 30.

39. "Memorial and Remonstrance Against Religious Establishments" par. 3 ("the same authority which can force a citizen to contribute three pence only of his property for the support of any one establishment, may force him to conform to any other establishment in all cases whatsoever").

40. Various drafts of the religion clauses are collected in Laycock, "'Nonpreferential' Aid to Religion," 879-82. For original sources, see Linda G. dePauw, ed., *Documentary History of the First Federal Congress of the United States of America* (Baltimore: Johns Hopkins University Press, 1972), 1:135, 151, 166, 181; ibid. 3:159, 166, 228; *Annals of Congress*, First Congress, 434 (8 June 1789); ibid., 729-31 (15 August 1789). Different printings of the *Annals of Congress* have different pagination; the date is a more reliable way to find particular passages.

41. Jonathan Elliot, ed., *The Debates in the Several State Conventions on the Adoption of the Federal Constitution*, 2d ed. (Philadelphia: J.B. Lippincott, 1836), 224, 328, 659.

42. *Annals of Congress*, First Congress, 729-31 (15 August 1789). This debate is more thoroughly analyzed in Laycock, "'Nonpreferential' Aid to Religion," 885-94.

43. See Smith, "Religion Clauses," 611, 613; Comment, "*Muller v. Allen* : Tuition Tax Relief and the Original Intent," *Harvard Journal of Law & Public Policy* 7 (1984):551, 573 n.124.

44. Gaustad, "Religion and Ratification," pp. 41-59. For other disparaging views of Rhode Island, see Curry, *First Freedoms*, 20-21, 91, 112, 183; McDonald, *Novus Ordo Seclorum*, 175-76.

45. *Annals of Congress*, First Congress, 730 (15 August 1789).

46. Ibid., 731 (15 August 1789).

47. See Cord, *Separation of Church and State*, 53-80, 261-70.

48. Daniel J. Boorstin, *The Americans: The Colonial Experience* (New York: Random House, 1958), 130-31.

49. Michael McConnell, "The Origins and Historical Understanding of

Free Exercise of Religion," *Harvard Law Review* 103 (May 1990):1409.

50. See Laycock, "Text, Intent, and the Religion Clauses."

51. See Laycock, "Formal, Substantive, and Disaggregated Neutrality Toward Religion," *DePaul Law Review*(1990) (forthcoming).

52. McConnell, *"Free Exercise of Religion,"* 1466-73.

53. See e.g., Conn. Const. art. 1, 3; Ga. Const. art. 1, 4; Md. Declaration of Rights art. 36; Mass. Const. part 1 art. 2; N.H. Const. part 1, art. 5.

54. See *Employment Division v. Smith, United States Law Week* 58 (17 April 1990).

5

Original Intent and the Quest for Comparable Consensus

JOHN F. WILSON

This essay proposes to explore the problem of original intent with respect to the religion clauses of the First Amendment on the basis of this author's commitment to critical historical scholarship.[1] It is obvious that "original intent" has become the "turf" of legal historians and specialists in constitutional history; Leonard Levy's five-hundred-page study makes that clear.[2] But the *concept* of "original intent" is so important and so problematic as to invite reflection well beyond its discussion in legal circles. Indeed, such a review demands exploration of the nature of American society and government at their founding as well as today.

The notion of original intent initially appears to be simple and straightforward because it suggests the innocent objective of recovering a purpose conceived and willed by the founders, or architects, of our government. This conjecture, however, is misleading, for a fundamental mistake has already occurred if the issue is framed in this way. For such an objective presupposes that collective behavior, or the action of groups, is properly described and represented on the analogy of individuals. Language codifies cultural patterns that surely model individuals as thinking and behaving creatures about whom it is appropriate to say: "He or she intends this or that." Of course, modern psychological perspectives may suggest that intention is certainly not always (and may never be) undivided or simple. But for purposes of conceiving individuals as subjects before the law, or as subjects of education, or as potential political subjects, in sum, as culturally constructed, one makes the general assumption that individuals are intending creatures. Thus it makes sense to say, so and so went on a trip to California to do such and such, or attended graduate school to achieve this objective, or in drafting a will purposed this or that outcome. Individuals, our culture assumes, should be conceived of as intending particular outcomes, and thus held responsible for determinate actions. American criminal law is based on such premises.

By the same token, it does not seem that within American culture the same claim is justified about collective purposes or objectives—conditions assumed in a discussion of original intent. Some might say such a high doctrine of group belief and behavior was what John Winthrop gave voice to in his lay sermon on the *Arabella* which talked of a "city on the hill." But apparently within his own lifetime Winthrop himself had begun to face the nonviability of *that* concept, and surely by the time of the revolutionary struggle against England's domination of her colonies a century and a half later, such corporate constructs were not current within the separate colonies, let alone common to them. To speak of intent in American culture as describing collective or corporate actions was from colonial times on, at the least, only rhetorical (designed to foster action) and at the most patently fictive (as such misrepresenting reality). So to speak as if the founding generation operated in terms of an original intent in any but the most general and metaphoric sense is a mistake in a critical analysis of the founding moment. Understanding our national beginnings is not served if such an approach to the past is allowed; it can only be sentimental or manipulative.

Beyond these preliminary considerations, much recent actual use of the concept "original intent" has been so manifestly political (in the sense of rising out of a desire to influence current policy and practice directly) that we must find it suspect from a scholarly viewpoint. Whether taking the cruder and more general sense apparently meant by the former attorney general, Edwin Meese, or in the more specific and nuanced sense espoused by Chief Justice William H. Rehnquist in reference to the religion clauses, its burden has been to force revision in the prevailing interpretations of them.[3] The ideal of original intent has been advanced and shaped for the purpose of forcing significant reconception of policy, not to speak of law. For these immediate reasons, then, it is necessary to subject the call for a jurisprudence of original intent to review and analysis, for it is being used to challenge directly a half-century of formal legal interpretation of the place of religion in the United States, which in turn developed from, and to some extent codified, a century and a half of informal practice in this area.

A critical historical perspective on the origins of the First Amendment religion clauses calls into question conventional assumptions about them. Typical interpretation of the clauses has made much of James Madison's role as the member of the first Congress who took up the burden of proposing a "Bill of Rights" to meet the Anti-Federalists' fears about the Constitution. So Madison as author of an initial draft, and probable participant in a conference committee between the houses, becomes the consciousness through which the text is interpreted. This trail leads the interpreter back into Madison's role in the Virginia struggle for religious disestablishment as a means of filling out the likely content of his proposals. His presumed intent, in part known from his earlier actions as a Virginian, is read as if it determined the fundamental meaning of

the clauses. And secondarily, his relationship to Thomas
Jefferson works to privilege the latter's point of view as defining
the clauses' true significance. Finally, in a tertiary sense,
occasional ex post facto actions of one or both, while each served
as president, or reflected on practices in their post presidential
lives, are taken as essentially definitive for interpretation of the
First Amendment clauses.

It is a mistake to attribute such precise interpretations to
these particular provisions in the Constitution. At least in
critical historical perspective we are better served by
understanding the texts as having satisfied larger objectives
widely shared, and by recognizing that compromises on
restricted and particular issues like the wording of these clauses
were required. Thus one might properly look for a consensus
that sets general objectives (an effective national government
that was federal in structure) and that surely favored certain
structural approaches (such as limiting power and constructing
checks and balances); but it is wrong to assume anything like
shared conscious intentions joined together to craft special
provisions or even the wording of particular clauses.

This is especially the case when, by explicit agreement, the
Constitutional Convention meeting in Philadelphia was
conducted in secret, so that no reliable record exists of what
went on where the most basic decision concerning religion was
struck, namely to make office holding in the proposed new
federal government independent of religious test oaths. With
respect to the First Amendment, we have a better sense of the
matter. But note that interpreting the texts must take account of
the following kinds of factors: the amorphous and complex
demands voiced by Anti-Federalists in the separate states to
which the first Congress only most reluctantly came to respond;
the tortuous passage through House and Senate deliberations in
the course of which markedly different texts were offered,
suggesting thereby basic disagreements over objectives and
purposes; the various courses of ratification in the several states,

about which there is extremely limited evidence; and the somewhat accidental grouping of ten amendments, of which the first one contingently collected together disparate provisions for "rights."

I am troubled by talk of "First Amendment freedoms" as if there were a manifest and luminous collective intention fully codified and expressed definitively in a text that has become canonical. Here several different perspectives on the same subject must be made explicit. In constitutional law there is one text (not several) of the Constitution and the First Amendment. Through the development of American polity there is provision for review and definitive interpretation of this text as specific needs arise. But that function of providing current determination of what the Constitution means in the context of the modern polity is not to be confused with a critical historical understanding of how the text came to be—or what original purposes it served.

The analogy seems very strong between, on the one hand, the Constitution and jurisprudence, and, on the other, sacred scripture and interpretation and application of its texts.[4] For the rabbi concerned with the Pentateuch, or the preacher/theologian concerned with the canonical New Testament, the text is the alpha and the omega. Its status may not put a stop to inquiries about where it comes from and what purposes it serves. What it does do most basically, however, is to provide a standard point of reference for an authoritative interpretation of policy in the current and continuing community for whose members it is the source of authority. Of course the modern rabbi or theologian may indeed be schooled in contemporary biblical criticism. And he or she may make use of the fruits of such work to seek to reinterpret the canonical text. But for the rabbi or theologian the authority lies in the *text*, not in the exploration of sources for the text or in comparative studies of it. For the critical scholar, however, the consuming interest is in just these questions of sources, circumstances, and purposes served by codification.

Thus the critical scholar's work may inform, but should not be confused with, the work of the rabbi or theologian, or by analogy the constitutional jurist. The quest for "original intent" has largely entailed a confusion of these approaches. Unfortunately, it has also been undertaken selectively with the goal of arguing that the demonstrated original purpose supports a partisan contemporary position. In consequence the work of critical scholarship has been wrongly construed and in part corrupted.

A useful starting point for another stage of this analysis is the observation that specialists in the law have become increasingly self-conscious about the *kinds of arguments* that have a place in American jurisprudence. A very ambitious discussion along these lines constitutes the core of Philip Bobbitt's *Constitutional Fate*.[5] In it he offers a typology of the basic arguments that form, as well as inform, the American legal tradition. He identifies six categories that together comprise distinct modes of legal reasoning in the American system. His pure types are the historical, textual, doctrinal, prudential, structural, and ethical. Indeed, he finally recognizes them as archetypal, believing that they synthesize in different combinations in actual legal reasoning. This essay does not presume to offer a critique of this typology, but the Bobbitt book, and other recent literature as well, forces to the fore the point that the conduct of law not only entails special kinds of reasoning, but that taken as a whole these comprise a family of reasonings that is distinct from other kinds of intellectual inquiries. In particular, historical reasoning in the law is not to be simply assimilated more generally to critical historical reasoning.

By critical historical scholarship in this case, I mean the sustained and self-conscious attempt to achieve understanding of the creation of the early United States as a new nation. For the sake of this discussion this author will argue that this enterprise is distinctive and has somewhat different characteristics from other modes of engagement with the past—in particular, that of the jurist, or the historian of law. To carry forward the comparison, for the jurist the objective is to explore historical materials as they bear on the application of texts to modern cases, while for the historian of law it is to trace development of that cultural tradition. For the critical historian, however, relevance to modern cases or to law as a cultural construct is not as significant as a satisfactory explanation of the text seen in relation to other relevant subjects, all in their social and cultural contexts. The convincing construction of evidence, in the broadest possible framework, is the critical historian's formal objective rather than demonstrated relevance to the present of a particular constitutional provision. Furthermore, in the perspective of critical historical scholarship, any relevance a subject may have to the present requires mediation through a construction of the present as comprehensive as that of the past. Thus society and culture as interrelated systems become the frames of reference for past and present alike. At the core, reasoning in the law as jurisprudence or as historiography is an exercise of practical reasoning, while the critical historical enterprise is one that entails significant theoretical reasoning.

In the law, historical reasoning traditionally focuses on a text, rehearsing the genesis of a particular clause or provision and establishing its meaning. Here the category "intent" means understanding how and why particular provisions of the Constitution came to be, e.g., what considerations and factors played into the crafting of the two religion clauses of the First Amendment—ranging from Madison's initial draft through modifications to the language finally ratified and "constitutionalized." Of course, this line of inquiry can, in principle, ramify very widely and deeply, seeking remote as well as more immediate and direct sources for the text of the Constitution. However, such historical reasoning in the law does not reach beyond such a terminus to inquiry. Leonard Levy's book is an exhibit on this point.

At least for the sake of discussion this author will propose that if in procedure and style such historical legal reasoning shares much with critical historical reasoning more generally, a very important distinction between them remains. Critical historical inquiry is not in the end limited by a formal terminal point of constitutional text or the law. Rather, it views the law in relationship to other cognate subjects: the political dynamics of a social system, analyses of economic factors, religious institutions, and movements; in short, the society and culture of which the law is a part only, however significant. Accordingly, critical historical reasoning is more a process or procedure without determinate outcomes or boundaries than historical inquiry in the law.

If, then, the question of original intent is viewed in the type of framework required by critical historiography, the quest expands well beyond specifically legal questions into theorizing about the nature of the national community as it formed and how it was governed, and finally into how politics as legitimated power relationships is currently understood. Furthermore, in the setting of critical historiography, insofar as attentiveness to original intent concerns the burden or weight properly placed upon the clauses today, such an undertaking requires that those clauses be interpreted in ways that are accepted as legitimate, less for reasons of narrow fidelity to text than their persuasiveness in light of broader theoretical issues and insistent practical considerations.

One means of reinforcing this basic point is to offer exhibits that illustrate how jurists, historians of law, and critical historians each work. Note the *kind* of language used by the Supreme Court as it interprets the Establishment Clause. First, Justice Hugo Black's classic delineation of its meaning in *Everson*.

The "establishment of religion" clause of the First Amendment means at least this: Neither a state nor the Federal Government can set up a church. Neither can pass laws which aid one religion, aid all religions, or prefer one religion over another. Neither can force nor influence a person to go to or to remain away from church against his will or force him to profess a belief or disbelief in any religion. No person can be punished for entertaining or professing religious beliefs or disbeliefs, for church attendance or non-attendance. No tax in any amount, large or small, can be levied to support any religious activities or institutions, whatever they may be called, or whatever form they may adopt to teach or practice religion. Neither a state nor the Federal Government can, openly or secretly, participate in the affairs of any religious organizations or groups and vice versa. In the words of Jefferson, the clause against establishment of religion by law was intended to erect "a wall of separation between Church and State."[6]

Place beside this Justice Rehnquist's counter-delineation in *Wallace v. Jaffree*, to be sure a dissenting opinion.

> It would seem from this evidence that the Establishment Clause of the First Amendment had acquired a well-accepted meaning: it forbade establishment of a national religion, and forbade preference among religious sects or denominations. . . . The Establishment Clause did not require government neutrality between religion and irreligion nor did it prohibit the federal government from providing non-discriminatory aid to religion. There is simply no historical foundation for the proposition that the Framers intended to build the "wall of separation" that was constitutionalized in *Everson*.[7]

Beyond their obvious disagreement in interpreting the same clause, both exhibit strikingly similar assumptions. Both positivistically assert that the clause had a relatively simple meaning and, furthermore, that it has direct and unproblematic application to the common life of the nation even two centuries after it was drafted, approved, and ratified.

This jurisprudential reasoning, as one might term it, provides a nice point of contrast to the mandate accepted by a constitutional historian. Leonard Levy's recent book on original intent provides a case in point. Here is a summary paragraph from his discussion of the Establishment Clause:

Several facts clearly emerge from the legislative history of the Establishment Clause. The United States had no authority prior to the First Amendment to enact laws about religion; only the states held that power. The amendment did not increase the legislative power of Congress. Congress seriously considered alternative readings of the Establishment Clause and rejected every phrasing that logic could construe as more narrow than the final version. The Livermore-New Hampshire alternative, the broadest restriction of power, failed because it did not mention an establishment. Another fact may be added: the meaning of an "establishment of religion" remains uncertain after an analysis of the legislative history. Whatever such an establishment was, the nation's legislature faced an absolute ban concerning it.[8]

Levy's description of the clause's legislative history operates at a different level from the statements offered by justices. While as a historian his focus remains on the clause that finally emerges, its problematic quality is immediately acknowledged. So the historian of law's inquiry, like that of the jurist's determination, is primarily oriented to the text that emerges, but the inquiry has no difficulty acknowledging either the ambiguous origins of the text in question or the modern necessity to interpret it.

By contrast to both jurisprudential reasoning and the work of the historian of law, there is the activity of critical historical studies. Here the subject is, so to speak, not the particular words of a text, nor the clause that emerged from an elaborate process, but finally the process itself, in this case the constitutionalizing of a nation from hitherto—however briefly—sovereign states. And the burden for a critical historian is making that founding moment intelligible. Two brief sections from Gordon Wood's magisterial *The Creation of the American Republic* may be helpful.

Americans had retained the forms of the Aristotelian schemes of government but had eliminated the substance, thus divesting the various parts of the government of their social constituents. Political power was thus disembodied and became essentially homogeneous. the division of this political power now became (in Jefferson's words) "the first principle of a good government." . . . Separation of powers . . . was simply a partitioning of political power, the creation of a plurality of discrete governmental elements, all detached from yet responsible to and controlled by the people, checking and balancing each other, preventing any one power from asserting itself too far. . . .

It was an imposing conception—a kinetic theory of politics—such a crumbling of political and social interests, such an atomization of authority, such a parceling of power, not only in the governmental institutions but in the extended sphere of the society itself, creating such a multiplicity and a scattering of designs and passions, so many checks, that no combination of parts could hold, no group of evil interests could long cohere. Yet out of the clashing and checking of this diversity Madison believed the public good, the true perfection of the whole, would somehow arise.[9]

Of course the adoption of specific language about religion in the Constitution and the Bill of Rights is only a minor part of that event. That some two centuries later courts interpret that language about the status of religion as still binding, however, derives from the fact that the American republic proved durable. Any less encompassing framework does not—as far as critical historical inquiry is concerned—go to the heart of the matter.

This moves this discussion to another stage. If it is wrong in principle to expect critical historical studies to establish the definitive interpretation of particular clauses (such as the religion clauses of the First Amendment) for purposes of modern usage, is there a way to bring together the fruits of critical scholarship and the judicial interpretation of texts? If the quest for the "original intent" of a clause is a mistake with respect to its psychological premises and a misappropriation of the project of critical historical investigation, is there a means of bringing together these separate endeavors that does not do violence to each activity? The only defensible strategy necessarily involves seeing specific texts in the context of broader considerations such as consensus on basic principles.

This strategic move suggests we ought to look for something like a collective consensus sustaining the founding of a new nation rather than particular intentions specific to a single or several concrete provisions. And we should look at the fundamental charter crafted to facilitate that outcome less in terms of the separate provisions it contains than in terms of the set of principles or polity it codifies. Thus the specific clauses should be viewed as expressions of underlying and contingent principles rather than as freestanding provisions in their own right. It is useful to take on each of these two hypotheses in turn since they involve, respectively, the issue of what *collective purposes* predominated in the founding of the nation and the issue of the *principles that gave coherence* to the instrument created to realize that goal.

For the first, the overriding collective purpose was surely that of achieving a government adequate for the new and struggling nation. Essentially the first government under the Articles was inadequate because its authority and power were insufficient to address certain issues, especially regulation of the economy in an expanding mercantilist context and provision for the common defense. To achieve this outcome would require that the sovereignty of the constituent states be qualified to some degree. So the broad design or consensus of the Constitutional Convention was to substitute a federal government which would draw its legitimacy both from the people at large and from the constituent states whose power, necessarily, would be circumscribed by it. Such a design further entailed constructing the legislative and executive branches so that both would be able to represent the continuing interests of the states and to use strategies such as dividing powers between the proposed branches of government. Here the nature of the electoral college and the original means of selecting senators are critical pieces of evidence about the underlying theories that were adopted to institutionalize the purpose.

In something of the same way, the federal government was to leave to the still-sovereign states authority to deal with numerous issues. Among such matters were important questions such as citizens' rights (including those concerned with religious liberty), the place of religious institutions, and a host of unenumerated issues whose potential relationship to the federal system has become clear only over time, for example, national interest in education, provisions for marriage, criminal justice codes, and eligibility to vote, among many others.

If one asks where this program finds fullest expression, surely the answer must be in the *Federalist Papers*, where something approaching a broad theoretical justification was worked out from the basic principles codified in the Constitution.[10] Parenthetically, Morton White's recent *Philosophy, the Federalist, and the Constitution* is a superb analysis of something that might be termed an original philosophical consensus on the polity.[11] Of course, critics of the new federal system—the Anti-Federalists—sensed the potential for this new government to reach beyond a minimalist construction of its powers by means of the reserved powers provision. But in retrospect such a prospect seems to have been exaggerated due to fears that the principle of balancing powers within the federal government, and between that government and the states, would not turn out to constitute a self-regulating system. Of course, without the luxury of isolation, which the new nation enjoyed for a century and more before it was drawn into sustained international engagement, this federal system might have proved unstable. Indeed, it did eventually prove unstable. How else are we to understand an internal war occasioned by slavery—one basic issue which was not resolved in the original consensus? The essence of that war was that the federal union

was contested. And the outcome of the Civil War surely made
newly relevant the old Anti-Federalist fear about centralization
of power. Fortunately the federal guarantee of individual civil
rights, however much of an afterthought in the first place, would
over time come to play a rather different role in bringing balance
to the system.

This essay has attempted to sketch out the level of generality
at which it is proper to look for an original consensus which may
suggest a "middle term" for addressing contemporary issues.
This level had to do with creating an adequate government that
would yet be in synergy with the states, the latter retaining
considerable authority in the new system. I believe that we must
interpret the first Amendment religion clauses and Article VI,
Section 3, of the Constitution too, in relationship to that
framework—or a more nuanced version of it if the critical enterprise is to continue its course. From the point of view of critical
scholarship, the theory of the Constitution is the correct
framework in which the text of the First Amendment should be
situated. By contrast, while the Virginia struggle to disestablish
the Church of England and to affirm religious freedom may illu-
minate brightly the place of the religious issue in *one* state prior
to the resolve to perfect the national government, and further
while it exhibits some then-current language in respect to these
matters, it does not properly provide much insight into the
federal provisions that played their roles in a very different
setting. On these principles, evidence from no other state would
be any better. Critical historical interpretation of these clauses,
then, must depend more upon imaginative review and
understanding of the Constitution and the government formed
under it than on exploring specific precedents or practices in the
states considered singly or taken together. (Jurists in their elaboration of the law may find these precedents and practices
weightier than historians.)

Where does this leave us with respect to the problem of the
return to "original intent"? The emphasis must be placed on the

distinction between the elaboration of law and the contribution of critical historical understanding. For the latter, the point is that in a vastly different polity, developed over the intervening two hundred years, relevant provisions (in this case the First Amendment religion clauses) must be seen in relation to the current structures of government, considered in terms of principles and their interpretation in practice. Originally, the federal program erected a system upon the basic principles of limiting government and dividing powers. Those principles remain central to modern American polity, albeit expressed in different and often unanticipated ways—through a two-party structure, for example. But specific constitutional provisions must continue to be interpreted in the light of these principles, that is to say, with reference to that level of generality. Of course, if other principles have displaced those that were fundamental at the outset, then the religion clauses will finally be made intelligible in *their* light.

In a sense, reconstruction of the Constitution goes on perpetually and in a piecemeal fashion in any case. But the jurist, or even the historian of law, has the burden of emphasizing continuity with the past even if, to borrow a scriptural figure, new wine is poured into old wineskins. The contribution of the critical historical enterprise has a different sort of bias: to highlight the disjunction, to emphasize the discontinuity between eras by analyzing the interpenetration of contemporary factors in any one era.

Distinguishing between the different purposes and procedures of the jurist and historian of law, on the one hand, and the work of a critical historian, on the other hand, and applying that distinction to interpretation of the religion clauses, has a very noteworthy outcome. Within the law as a system, jurisprudence has come to emphasize the positive role of the First Amendment clauses, indeed the priority given to protection of conscience against state assault as basic to all the freedoms secured in the Constitution. Indeed, given the expanding commitment to rights under the modern national government, this is logical and compelling in the process of working out the presuppositions of a pluralistic culture. But note that this principle, that the federal government guarantees individual rights, is relatively recent.[12] In the modern Constitution, as the national government has become the guarantor of rights, the other principles of the Constitution have inevitably been affected. Indeed, the compromise of federalism and readjustment of the division of powers has inevitably followed this enhanced national role in the guarantee of individual rights. In the work of critical historiography, one must note the kaleidoscopic shift in the modern construction of the religion clauses. From being quintessential expressions of the principles of federalism and exhibits of how national power was limited, they have come to embody the national guarantee of rights, and as such represent a net reduction of federalism and an enhancement of central powers—remote indeed from any original intent in any ordinary sense.

Where does this leave us? This author contends that while jurists and historians of law should, indeed must, ground contemporary applications of the religion clauses in the Constitution and its development, critical historical scholars may have a different (but related) role to play. This is to emphasize the cultural distance between 1789 and 1989. By cultural distance is meant the fundamental differences between the nation as founded and the nation near the end of the twentieth century. These differences surely involve such issues as a vaster scale of territory and compression of time, both achieved through technology. They also involve such changes as urban growth, the industrial transformations, and the variety of peoples who have made the nation their home. Finally, they involve the markedly changed principles from which Americans understand their government functions: subordination of the states; enhancement of relatively independent corporate power to operate the economy; direct, extensive interaction of citizens with agencies of the national government; and shifting coalitions of interests both within and outside formal governmental organizations. These and other differences sum to a particular kind of modern state operating on principles of government that are not necessarily wholly recognized. But this reconfiguration of our society and its culture must provide the framework of intelligibility for how religion as beliefs, practices, institutions, and meanings will be respected and regulated. This is the *real* agenda, demythologized or without clothes, so to speak, that in a mythic or veiled form jurists and historians of law pursue in their resolve to emphasize the law's continuity. Of course, the mode of their operation is precisely to claim legitimacy for the necessarily recast formulations.

What is the moral of this exercise? That the relentless pursuit by critical scholarship of "original intent," for instance, with respect to the religion clauses, in the end only emphasizes how much the clauses were woven into the fabric of the society that crafted the Constitution. In recognizing the new fabric that sustains contemporary American society in our era, it is clear that if these clauses are to have significance today they must express the current fundamental operating principles of the society. Now they must speak to the essential pluralism of our culture, which exists in tension with a powerful modern state. So their burden must be to support the rights of conscience, and to limit the scope of governmental power over collective and individual religious actions. Are these related to an original consensus they may have rested on? Of course. But their roles today are very different indeed, for they were originally cast to preserve the authority of the states over religion and to limit the reach of the new government. Now the authority of the federal state shields religion (collective and individual, behavior and belief) from intrusions of state and local regimes as well as of the federal government.

Indeed, if pressed to identify the real pay-off of this line of inquiry, it can be formulated as follows. Through its two

hundred years, the nation has come to be governed by a modern
state in which the basic principles of dividing and separating
powers on the one hand, and checks and balances on the other,
have remained, but their operation, their reality, has become
very different. As the constituent states have lost power, the
related federal framework, so carefully constructed, has been
stretched—possibly to the breaking point. One of the most
important modern functional equivalents to early federalism is
cultural pluralism. And the cultural pluralism of the
contemporary United States has no greater constitutional
bulwark than the provisions guaranteeing space for religious
diversity in our society. Thus, while jurisprudential reasoning
may interpret the constitutional text to function in that way, and
while historical analysis by legal scholars may help ground relevant reasoning to that end, only a critical historical framework
provides understanding of what has in fact transpired. In this
sense, if the quest for original intent by critical historians has
anything to contribute, it will be the insistence that such a quest
be recast into a search for what we might term a comparable
consensus.

Why has this essay mounted this elaborate argument, that
some may say is totally convoluted and wrongheaded?
Certainly not because jurisprudential reasoning should change;
nor because the author fails to appreciate the impressive work of
legal historians. Rather, it is only by taking on the issue of
religion and the Constitution *at its most general level* can one
finally acknowledge both the contingent nature of the American
political system—it could have taken a very different form—and
that precious rights like those relating to religion must finally be
won again by each generation. How else can one make sense of
aspects of American history in which the Constitution was make
complicitous with evil? It ought to be a salutary reminder that
while the Declaration of Independence—and also the "Virginia
Memorial and Remonstrance," for that matter—proclaimed life
and liberty as natural rights, the Constitution saw fit to deny

political liberty to slaves. In the same way that it took political resolve even to the point of enduring a Civil War correctly to develop the implications of the new nation chartered in the Constitution, political resolve alone can preserve such liberties as Americans cherish with respect to religion.

While the clauses and the courts may constitutionalize religious freedom, it is the political culture that must preserve it through continuously reauthorizing the ideal of religion as independent of government, in turn that will sustain the necessary interpretation of the clauses which will make that independence real. This is the level at which the original consensus must have its resonance in these times if this democratic republic is to survive. I am reluctant to claim that critical historians should set out to help save the nation, but that could be a by-product of such endeavors!

NOTES

1. A growing literature explores the questions addressed in this essay. Among very recent publications see especially essays by David A. J. Richards, "Founders' Intent and Constitutional Interpretation" (26-52) and John Sexton, "Of Walls, Gardens, Wildernesses, and Original Intent: Religion and the First Amendment" (84-109) in Leslie Berlowitz, Denis Donoghue, and Louis Menard, eds., *America in Theory* (New York: Oxford University Press, 1988). Douglas Laycock is also writing widely on these themes.

2. Leonard W. Levy, *Original Intent and the Framers' Constitution* (New York: Macmillan, 1988).

3. Chief Justice Rehnquist, writing in his dissent in *Wallace v. Jaffree*, 472 U.S. 38 (1985).

4. Michael Perry has explored these analogies. See especially his article "The Authority of Text, Tradition, and Reason: A Theory of Constitutional 'Interpretation,'" *Southern California Law Review* 58 (1985): 551.

5. Philip Bobbitt, *Constitutional Fate* (New York: Oxford University Press, 1982).

6. *Everson v. Board of Education*, 330 U.S. 1 (1947) at 15,16.

7. *Wallace* at 106.

8. Levy, *Original Intent*, 182-83.

9. Gordon S. Wood, *The Creation of the American Republic, 1776-1787* (New York: W. W. Norton & Company, 1972), 604-05.

10. While "Publius" represented the pens of Alexander Hamilton, John Jay, and James Madison; Hamilton and Madison carried the burden. In general, Madison tended to address theoretical issues while Hamilton discussed the structural arrangements proposed for the new government.

11. Morton White, *Philosophy, the Federalist, and the Constitution* (New York: Oxford University Press, 1987).

12. It dates with respect to the religion clauses of the First Amendment from *Cantwell v. Connecticut*, 310 U.S. 296 (1940) and *Everson v. Board of Education*, 330 U.S. 1 (1947).

6

The Unity of the First Amendment Religion Clauses

LEO PFEFFER

In March of 1980, the *Minnesota Law Review*[1] published an article by the author of this essay entitled "Freedom and/or Separation: The Constitutional Dilemma of the First Amendment." Its premise was that the religion clauses of the First Amendment[2] encompassed a unitary guaranty of separation and freedom. This was not the first time he had made this suggestion. In his chapter entitled "The Case for Separation" in *Religion in America,* published in 1958, he had said: "Separation and freedom are not separate concepts or principles but really two sides of a single coin. The fathers of the First Amendment were convinced that the free exercise of religion and the separation of church and state were two ways of saying the same thing: that separation guaranteed freedom and freedom required separation."[3]

He was by no means the only person to hold this position. Professor Philip Kurland of the University of Chicago, in a 1961 article,[4] later extended into a book,[5] proposed a thesis that the

ban in the First Amendment on laws respecting an establishment
of religion or prohibiting its free exercise was a single, unitary
mandate of stark neutrality, which equally prohibited laws
favoring religion and those enjoining it. Towards the end of the
book he summarized his position in the following words: "The
freedom and separation clauses should be read as stating a
single precept: that government cannot utilize religion as a
standard for action or inaction because these clauses, read
together as they should be, prohibit classification in terms of religion either to confer a benefit or to impose a burden."[6] In short,
the First Amendment required government to be "religion-blind"
as the Fourteenth required it to be color-blind. Not everyone
agreed with Kurland. Indeed, there were substantially more
who disagreed than agreed. The following is from an article by
Bette Novit Evans that appeared in the Autumn 1988 issue of
Journal of Church and State: "Two decades ago, constitutional
scholar Philip B. Kurland argued that the combined meaning of
the two clauses was to render the constitution religion-blind;
religion could be used to grant neither benefits nor burdens. His
completely secular understanding of the two clauses captured
some of the spirit of the era, but ultimately proved incapable of
offering sufficient free exercise protections."[7] This statement
obviously assumes a basic separateness of the Establishment and
Free Exercise Clauses of the First Amendment.

Yet there was ample evidence to support the view of the
unity of the religion clauses. In *Everson v. Board of Education*
Justice Wiley Rutledge (dissenting from a majority opinion
upholding use of tax-raised funds to finance bus transportation
to parochial schools) said: "'Establishment' and 'free exercise'
were correlative and coextensive ideas, representing only different facets of the single great and fundamental freedom."[8] The
history that led up to the adoption of the First Amendment fully
supported Justice Rutledge's conclusion. Roger Williams, for
example, opposed an "enforced uniformity of religion" (freedom
concept) because it "confounds the Civil and Religious"

(separation concept).[9] James Madison opposed a bill establishing a provision for teachers of the Christian religion (separation concept) because it violated the "fundamental and undeniable truth, 'that religion . . . can be directed only by reason and conviction, not by force or violence'" (freedom concept).[10] Virginia's Act for Establishing Religious Freedom was adopted in 1786 because of "the impious presumption of legislators and rulers" who had "established and maintained false religions" (separation concept).[11] In *Common Sense,* Thomas Paine noted the unity of the dualism: "As to religion," he wrote, "I hold it to be the indispensable duty of every government, to protect all conscientious professors thereof, and I know of no other business which government hath to do therewith."[12]

The initial version of the First Amendment, submitted by James Madison for consideration by Congress, stated, "The civil rights of none shall be abridged on account of religious belief or worship, nor shall any national religion be established, nor shall the full and equal rights of conscience be in any manner, nor on any pretext, infringed."[13] President Thomas Jefferson refused to proclaim days of fasting and prayer because of "the provision that no law shall be made respecting the establishment, or free exercise of religion."[14]

In an 1878 case involving a *freedom clause* attack on an antipolygamy statute, the Supreme Court quoted Jefferson's "Letter to the Baptists" which explicitly stated that the First Amendment was intended to erect "a wall of *separation* between church and state."[15]

In 1889 James Bryce wrote: "It is accepted as an axiom by all Americans that civil power ought to be not only neutral and impartial as between different forms of faith, but ought to leave these matters entirely on one side, regarding them no more than it regards the artistic or literary pursuits of the citizens. There seem to be no two opinions on this subject in the United States."[16]

Also to be recognized is the following paragraph from the writings of Jeremiah Black, a distinguished chief justice of Pennsylvania in the nineteenth century:

The manifest object of the men who framed the institutions of this country, was to have a *State without religion,* and a *Church without politics*—that is to say, they meant that one should never be used as an engine for any purpose of the other, and that no man's rights in one should be tested by his opinions about the other. As the Church takes no note of men's political differences, so the State looks with equal eye on all the modes of religious faith. . . . Our fathers seem to have been perfectly sincere in their belief that the members of the Church would be more patriotic, and the citizens of the State more religious, by keeping their respective functions entirely separate."[17]

Moreover, there are basic textual difficulties with the claim that the establishment and free exercise provisions reflect independent mandates which may conflict with each other. The First Amendment does not guarantee "the free exercise of religion"; it guarantees the free exercise of "thereof." As stated in Justice Rutledge's dissenting opinion in *Everson,* "'Religion' appears only once in the Amendment. But the word governs two prohibitions and governs them alike. It does not have two meanings, one narrow to forbid 'an establishment' and another, much broader, for securing 'the free exercise thereof.' 'Thereof' brings down 'religion' with its entire and exact content, no more and no less, from the first into the second guaranty, so that Congress and now the states are as broadly restricted concerning the one as they are regarding the other."[18] On this point, there was no disagreement with it on the Court in Justice Hugo Black's majority opinion in *Everson as cited in the previous essay, but here needs to be cited again.* It reads:

The "establishment of religion" clause of the First Amendment means at least this: Neither a state nor the Federal Government can set up a church. Neither can pass laws which aid one religion, aid all religions, or prefer one religion over another. *Neither can force* nor influence a person to go to or remain away from church *against his will* or *force him to profess a belief or disbelief* in any religion. *No person can be punished for entertaining or professing religious beliefs or disbeliefs, for church attendance or non-attendance.* No tax in any amount, large or small, can be levied to support any religious activities or institutions, whatever they may be called, or whatever form they may adopt to teach or practice religion. Neither a state nor the Federal Government can, openly or secretly, participate in the affairs of any religious organizations or groups and vice versa. In the words of Jefferson, the clause against establishment of religion by law was intended to erect "a wall of separation between Church and State."[19]

The emphasized material is obviously more relevant to free exercise rather than establishment, were they to be divided.

This association of coercion with establishment as well as free exercise appeared again in *Zorach v. Clauson*.[20] That case involved a released time statute enabling pupils whose parents so requested, to leave school an hour early each week to participate in religious instruction off school premises,[21] but did not extend it to encompass pupils whose parents wanted them to take music or art instruction even if not available at the school. In particular, the New York statute required releasing the pupils to a "duly constituted religious body." But on sharp questioning by the Justices during argument, counsel for the New York City Board of Education said that it would allow released pupils to receive religious instruction even from their parents at home.[22] Indeed, in light of later cases such as those relating to military service, unemployment compensation, and similar ones discussed later in this essay, it could hardly do otherwise. If that be the case, it would not be difficult to have the music or art teacher be at the pupil's home during released time periods. On that view of the facts, the Court not surprisingly upheld the statute.

Writing for the Court, Justice William O. Douglas rejected any issue of the free exercise of religion as "obtuse reasoning," because no one was "forced to go to the religious classroom." He continued, "If in fact coercion were used, if it were established that any one or more teachers were using their office to persuade or force students to take religious instruction, a wholly different case would be presented."[23] He then went on to base his ruling on the Establishment Clause issue on the same ground: "Moreover, apart from that claim of coercion, we do not see how New York by this type of 'released time' program has made a law respecting an establishment of religion within the meaning of the First Amendment."[24]

In fact coercion was used, and very much so, but the evidence did not reach the Court for what can only be called a pure technicality.[25] It is noteworthy, though, that the Court deemed the question to relate equally to free exercise and to establishment.

Two final notes relating to *Zorach* are relevant here and both are to be found in the closing sentences of the opinion: "Here, as we have said, the public schools do no more than accommodate their schedules to a program of outside religious instruction. [This is constitutional] unless separation of Church and State means that public institutions can make no adjustments to their schedules to accommodate the religious needs of the people. We cannot read into the Bill of Rights such a philosophy of hostility to religion."[26] The first deals with the creation of a new concept that has become very much relevant to church-state law, the concept of accommodation.[27] The second is the concluding sentence of the decision which equalizes opposition to the challenged statute with "hostility to religion"—this though both plaintiffs sent their children to religious schools for instruction at times other than during the public school day: the plaintiff,

Tessim Zorach, to an Episcopal church, the co-plaintiff, Esta Gluck, to a Jewish religious school.[28]

In the 1971 case of *Lemon v. Kurtzman*,[29] and all Establishment Clause cases but one thereafter,[30] the Court used the purpose-effect-entanglement formula. It reads: "First, the statute must have a secular legislative purpose; second, its principal or primary effect must be one that neither advances nor inhibits religion; finally, the statute must not 'foster an excessive government entanglement with religion.'" A ban on inhibiting religion obviously means the same as a ban on prohibiting the free exercise thereof.

Although the wording of *Everson* and *Lemon* differ, both are still the law of the land, and while purpose-effect-entanglement is now the usual formula in church-state cases, the no-aid of *Everson*, or perhaps more realistically of *McCollum*, is often also invoked and has never been considered obsolete.[31]

Finally, the fact that today all fifty states guarantee religious freedom and not one allows an establishment of religion would appear to be convincing evidence that in the American tradition the concepts of free exercise and nonestablishment are correlative and unitary.

THE UNITY CHALLENGED

To be sure, this principle of unity has not gone unchallenged. Some scholars have maintained that separation and free exercise were inherently different and the former was subordinate to the latter. In the words of Wilber Katz: "The principle of church-state separation is an instrumental principle. Separation ordinarily promotes religious freedom; it is defensible so long as it does so, and only so long."[32] Similarly, in his influential treatise, *American Constitutional Law*, Professor Laurence Tribe, after noting that "to the Framers, the religion clauses were at least compatible and at best mutually supportive," went on to assert that "serious tension has often surfaced between the two clauses." In such an event, he said, "the free exercise principle should be dominant in any conflict with the anti-establishment principle."[33]

In a 1980 paper this writer suggested that "although the Supreme Court has stated that there may be instances in which the establishment and free exercise clauses conflict with each other, the Court will continue to find ways to decide such cases without definitely adjudicating which clause is superior and which subordinate, or which must be preserved and which sacrificed."[34] The question proposed to be dealt with here is whether the situation in respect to establishment/free exercise has in reality changed in the 1980s.

It is probably true that in the 1980s decade the Supreme Court and individual Justices have more frequently referred to possible conflicts between the establishment and free exercise wings of the religion clause than ever before. (And it is true that the situation in respect to the Supreme Court's personnel has changed radically; President Ronald Reagan made no secret of his intent to convert what he called a radically liberal Court into a conservative one.) It is here suggested, however, that, as will be seen, the Court has continued to avoid a direct holding recognizing a conflict and choosing between establishment and free exercise.

The position that the Establishment and Free Exercise Clauses are separate entities gives rise to two types of situations for judicial determination. The first relates to cases where the plaintiff claims that the defendant has violated both the Establishment and the Free Exercises Clauses; the second relates to those wherein the parties present conflicting claims.

PLAINTIFFS INVOKING BOTH CLAIMS

In almost numberless cases plaintiffs will invoke both clauses; after all what have they got to lose? *Larson v. Valente*[35] is one of these. The case involved an amendment to Minnesota's Charitable Solicitation Act adopted to get rid of the Unification Church and other "cults." The statute required registration and financial reporting (which incorporated costs of management, fundraising, and public education and their transfers of property or funds out of the state, along with a designation of the recipients and the purposes of those transfers) only by religious organizations more than half of whose funds were obtained from non-members. The regular churches were thus exempt, but the "cults" were not. The Unification Church and some of its members challenged the law on both establishment and free exercise grounds.

In an opinion by Justice William J. Brennan the Court ruled that the statute violated the Establishment Clause principle under which one religious denomination cannot be officially preferred over another. Although the Court did not find it necessary to rule directly on the free exercise claim, Brennan did add that "this constitutional prohibition of denominational preferences is inextricably connected with the continuing vitality of the Free Exercise Clause."[36] Here, thus, the Court saw no conflict between the two clauses.

As recently as June 1989, the Court was again met with the problem of a challenge by a "cult," this time the Church of Scientology. Relevant to this article was a case in which both establishment and free exercise claims (among others) were invoked. The suit, *Hernandez v. Commissioner of Internal Revenue*,[37] involved Section 170 of the Internal Revenue Code which permits a taxpayer to deduct from gross income the amount of a "charitable contribution," a term defined in the statute to encompass entities organized and operated exclusively for religious purposes. The question presented to the Court was whether taxpayers may deduct as charitable contributions payments made to branches of the Church of Scientology in order to receive services known as "auditing" and "training." Under the practices of the Church an electronic device, named by the Church the E-meter, is used to help identification of the

areas of spiritual difficulty by measuring skin responses during a
question and answer session.[38]

Unfortunately, for the Church of Scientology, the decision
went against the Church. In a five-to-two opinion written by
Justice Thurgood Marshall (neither Justices Brennan nor
Anthony M. Kennedy participated in consideration of the case)
the Court, applying the tripartite *Lemon* test, upheld the decision
of the Internal Revenue Service in denying to Hernandez a tax
deduction. There was no allegation that the purpose of Section
170 was anti-religion or anti-Scientology. Nor was its primary
effect to advance or inhibit religion; nor was there an impermissible excessive entanglement between church and state. Routine
regulatory interaction, said the Court, which involved no
inquiries into religious doctrine, no delegation of state power to
a religious body, and no detailed monitoring and close adminis-
trative contact between secular and religious bodies, did not
create excessive entanglement.

As for the Free Exercise Clause, here, too, there was no
constitutional violation. The opinion cited *United States v. Lee*,[39]
in which the Court had rejected an Amish taxpayer's claim that
the Free Exercise Clause commanded his exemption from Social
Security tax obligations. There the Court noted that the tax
system could not function if denominations were allowed to
challenge the tax system on the ground that it operated in a
manner that violated their religious beliefs, and the same was
true in respect to the Church of Scientology.

Plaintiffs had unsuccessfully raised both free exercise and
establishment arguments in another tax case, *Bob Jones University
v. United States.*[40] In 1970 the Internal Revenue Service had
revised its policies to deny tax exemption to private schools with
racially discriminatory admission practices. Two religious
schools contended that this denial could not constitutionally be
extended to schools whose discriminatory policies were based
on sincere religious beliefs. The Supreme Court held, in an
opinion by Chief Justice Warren E. Burger that was unanimous

on this point, that the schools had legitimate rights under the Free Exercise Clause which could only be overcome by a compelling governmental interest, but that the effort to eradicate racial discrimination in education did meet that test. In a footnote the Court also rejected the claim that the IRS policy violated the Establishment Clause by preferring religions that do not believe in racial discrimination over ones that do. It noted that "a regulation does not violate the Establishment Clause merely because it 'happens to coincide or harmonize with the tenets of some or all religions.'"[41]

Another instance in which plaintiffs relied on both clauses is *Harris v. McRae*.[42] Involved in the case was a challenge to the constitutionality of an amendment to the Social Security Act which severely limited the use of federal Medicaid funds to reimburse the cost of abortions. The plaintiffs contended, among other things, that the amendment established a religious doctrine opposing abortion, and in addition restricted the religious liberty of women who wanted abortions for religious reasons. In particular, they argued that "insofar as a woman's decision to seek a medically necessary abortion may be a product of her religious beliefs under certain Protestant and Jewish tenets, [plaintiffs] assert that the funding limitations . . . impinge on the freedom of religion guaranteed by the Free Exercise Clause."[43] This might occur, for instance, if the abortion might or might not be necessary to save the life of the woman, in which case many, if not most ministers and rabbis would deem it sinful *not* to authorize an abortion. The trial court upheld the statute in respect to the Establishment Clause challenge but ruled it unconstitutional by reason of the Equal Protection and Free Exercise Clauses. The Supreme Court affirmed on Establishment, reversed as to Equal Protection and did neither as to Free Exercise. The reason for the last was that none of the named plaintiffs had standing to challenge the statute on Free Exercise grounds because the only plaintiffs who claimed to hold such religious beliefs did not allege that they were or might become pregnant and would be eligible to receive Medicaid.

Establishment and Free Exercise claims again came to the Supreme Court in the 1985 case of *Tony and Susan Alamo Foundation v. Secretary of Labor.*[44] The foundation was a nonprofit religious organization that received its income largely from the operation of commercial businesses by drug addicts, derelicts, or criminals after they were rehabilitated by the foundation. The workers received no cash salaries, but they were provided food, clothing, shelter, and other benefits. The U.S. Department of Labor, on its own and against the wishes of the workers (several testified that the concept of wages was against their religious tenets) designated them as "employees" within the meaning of the Fair Labor Standards Act; the workers, therefore, had to be paid the minimum amounts fixed by that law.

The foundation asserted both Free Exercise and Establishment claims, but prevailed in neither. With respect to free exercise, "it is," said Justice Byron R. White for a unanimous Court, "virtually self-evident that the Free Exercise Clause does not require an exemption from a governmental program [such as the Fair Labor Standards Act] unless, at a minimum, inclusion in the program actually burdens the claimant's freedom to exercise religious rights," which was not the case here because the employees could always voluntarily return their wages to the foundation.[45] As for the Establishment Clause argument, merely requiring the foundation to keep ordinary business records for its commercial activities was hardly excessive governmental entanglement with religion.[46]

ALLEGED, PURPORTED, AND POTENTIAL CONFLICTS

It is not entirely surprising that, in instances where the parties do not argue that there is a conflict between the Establishment and Free Exercise Clauses, the Supreme Court does not find one. The more searching test of the thesis of this essay is the Court's reaction to cases in which at least a potential conflict between the two clauses exists. Such cases will be examined.

Wisconsin v. Yoder[47] did not involve a conflict between Establishment and Free Exercise, although a statement in the Court's opinion by Chief Justice Burger would at first glance seem to suggest that it did. The case involved a compulsory school attendance law affecting pupils between the ages of seven and sixteen. The religious conscience of Old Order Amish parents forbids them to send their children to school after their completion of the eighth grade lest the salvation of both parents and children be adversely affected.

As set forth in the writ of certiorari to the Supreme Court the issue in controversy was the Free Exercise Clause. With only Justice Douglas dissenting, the Court held that the non-complying parents could not be constitutionally penalized under the terms of the statute: "The essence of all that has been said and written on the subject [said Burger] is that only those interests of the highest order and those not otherwise served can overbalance legitimate claims to the free exercise of religion."[48] What evoked an apparent conflict between Establishment and Free Exercise was the following sentence: "The Court must not ignore the danger that an exception from a general obligation of citizenship on religious grounds may run afoul of the Establishment Clause, but that danger cannot be allowed to prevent any exception no matter how vital it may be to the protection of values promoted by the right of free exercise."[49]

To support this, Chief Justice Burger quoted the following from *Walz v. Tax Commissioner*: "We have been able to chart a course that preserved the autonomy and freedom of religious bodies while avoiding any semblance of established religion. This is a 'tight rope' and one we have successfully traversed."[50] Returning to *Yoder* and the Establishment Clause, it should be noted that notwithstanding the above quotation, the Court went on to state expressly the following:

What we have said should meet the suggestion that the decision of the Wisconsin Supreme Court recognizing an exemption for the Amish from the State's system of compulsory education constituted an impermissible establishment of religion. In *Walz v. Tax Commission*, the Court saw the three main concerns against which the Establishment Clause sought to protect as "sponsorship, financial support and active involvement of the sovereign in religious activity." Accommodating the religious beliefs of the Amish can hardly be characterized as sponsorship or active involvement.[51]

Wisconsin v. Yoder did not present an establishment versus free exercise controversy for the simple reason that there was no establishment violation. The purpose of a statute requiring school attendance through the sixteenth year is, at least in major part, to prepare the child for adult living in the general modern society; the purpose is entirely different when the child is being prepared for life in the separated agrarian community that is the keystone of the Amish faith.

Among the more interesting cases in terms of the relationship between the Establishment and Free Exercise Clauses that have come to the Supreme Court are the series of decisions dealing with the question of whether a person whose religious beliefs forbid working on the Sabbath (usually, but not always, meaning Saturday) must, or may but must not, or may not at all, receive unemployment insurance benefits after rejecting an offer of a Sabbath-working job. It would seem that this situation presents a classic confrontation between the Free Exercise Clause rights of the Sabbath-observing employee and the Establishment Clause limitations, if not bans on preferential treatment to the religious believers but denies it to non-believers. The Court, though, has not seen the cases that way.

This issue first reached the Court as far back as 1952 in the case of *Heisler v. Board of Review*.[52] There a Jewish woman was denied unemployment benefits because her religious beliefs had led her to reject a job requiring her to work on Saturday. Her counsel, the author of this essay, tried to appeal the case to the Supreme Court claiming that denial violated both the Free Exercise and the Establishment Clauses (the latter because the law discriminated in favor of Sunday-observing religions). The Court (without dissent) dismissed the appeal for want of a substantial federal question, which was a ruling on the merits against her claim (i.e., that her case was so clearly without merit, there was no purpose in listening to her counsel's arguments), even though there was no Court precedent on the issue.[53]

In 1963, the Court, in *Sherbert v. Verner*,[54] held in an opinion by Justice Brennan, that not only did a claim of this sort raise a substantial federal question, but required a judgment that denial was constitutionally incorrect. (Not in the prevailing opinion nor in Justice Douglas' concurring opinion nor that of Justice Potter Stewart nor of Justice John M. Harlan's dissenting opinion was there any mention of *Heisler*.)

The disqualification for benefits, said Justice Brennan, speaking for a majority of the Court, imposed a burden on Ms. Sherbert's right to the free exercise of religion, since she had been required "to choose between following the precepts of her religion and forfeiting benefits, on the one hand, and abandoning one of the precepts of her religion in order to accept work, on the other hand. Government imposition of such a choice [he continued] puts the same kind of burden upon the free exercise of religion as would a fine imposed against appellant for her Saturday worship."[55]

At practically the very end of the opinion, Justice Brennan reached and disposed of in one sentence the subject of the Establishment Clause versus the Free Exercise Clause, with which this essay is concerned.

In holding as we do, plainly we are not fostering the "establishment" of Seventh-day Adventist religion in South Carolina, for the extension of unemployment benefits to Sabbatarians in common with Sunday worshippers reflects nothing more than the governmental obligation of neutrality in the face of religious differences, and does not represent that involvement of religious with secular institutions which it is the object of the Establishment Clause to forestall.[56]

Justice Stewart, who concurred in the result, the case involved a head-on collision between a legitimate claim under the Free Exercise Clause and the Court's prior "sterile construction of the Establishment Clause," from which Justice Stewart had dissented. He agreed that the law violated the Free Exercise Clause, but, the Establishment Clause as construed by the Court, he said, "not only *permits* but affirmatively *requires* South Carolina equally to deny the appellant's claim for unemployment compensation when her refusal to work on Saturday is based upon her religious creed. . . . To require South Carolina to so administer its law as to pay public money to the appellant under the circumstances of this case is thus clearly to require the State to violate the Establishment Clause as construed by this Court."[57]

Sherbert has had many progeny since it was decided, although the first of them, *In re Jenison*,[58] did not deal directly with Sabbath observance. A few months after the *Sherbert* decision, Jenison was held in contempt for refusing to serve on a Minnesota jury because the Bible commanded, "Judge not that ye be not judged." The Supreme Court set the decision aside for reconsideration in light of *Sherbert*. On reconsideration, the Minnesota court reversed itself and held that her refusal to serve on a jury did not constitute a grave danger to the administration of justice and therefore had to be accepted.[59]

The second case, *Thomas v. Review Board of Indiana*,[60] also did not deal with Sabbath observance. Eddie Thomas was a Jehovah's Witness who worked at a foundry and machinery company which fabricated sheet steel for a variety of industrial uses. When the roll foundry was closed, he was transferred to a department that produced turrets for military tanks. Thomas decided that such work violated Witness proscriptions (although other Witnesses were willing to work there), and asked to be laid off. When that request was denied, he quit and applied for unemployment compensation benefits under the Indiana Employment Security Act.

The Indiana Supreme Court held that he had left his job voluntarily for personal reasons and therefore was not eligible for unemployment compensation. Rejecting his claim under the Free Exercise Clause, that court said that denying Thomas benefits would create no more than an indirect burden on his Free Exercise rights. It also said that to award compensation benefits to a person who voluntarily terminates employment for religious reasons, while denying such benefits to persons who terminate for other personal but not religious reasons, would violate the Establishment Clause.

In an opinion by Chief Justice Burger the Supreme Court held that the denial of benefits violated the Free Exercise Clause. Religious beliefs, he said, need not be acceptable, logical, consistent, or comprehensible to others in order to merit First Amendment protection. Nor did it matter that other Jehovah's Witnesses interpreted their doctrine differently from Thomas. It was not for the courts to resolve such disputes, but only to adjudge the adherent's sincerity.

The Chief Justice did not devote much analysis to the Establishment Clause defense: "There is, in a sense, [he said] a 'benefit' to Thomas's deriving from his religious beliefs, but this manifests no more than the tension between the two Religious Clauses which the Court resolved in *Sherbert*."[61]

To Justice William H. Rehnquist, the only dissenter, the Court had gone astray in interpreting the Free Exercise and Establishment Clauses. He repeated and endorsed Justice Stewart's remarks in *Sherbert* that the decision was incompatible with the Court's Establishment Clause decisions. Unlike Justice Stewart, however, he thought *Sherbert* was wrong on the Free Exercise Clause as well, and he would have upheld the law.

In 1985 the Court decided *Estate of Thornton v. Caldor, Inc.,*[62] a case differing from all the others heretofore considered in this article in that the Sabbath involved was not that of Saturday, but Sunday. Donald Thornton, a Presbyterian, began working for the defendant, a department store chain, at a time when the Connecticut Sunday laws prevented the store from opening on that day. When the Sunday law was repealed, Thornton was assigned to work on Sundays. At first he complied. When he later objected on religious grounds to continuing to do so, he was reassigned to a less desirable position, from which he resigned. He did not, however, seek unemployment compensation, but rather challenged his reassignment under a Connecticut law which stated that "no person who states that a particular day of the week is observed as his Sabbath may be required by his employer to work on such day. An employee's refusal to work on his Sabbath shall not constitute grounds for his dismissal."

Affirming the state's decision adjudging the statute unconstitutional under the Establishment Clause, Chief Justice Burger opened his analysis as follows: "Under the Religion Clauses, government must guard against activity that impinges on religious freedom, and must take pains not to compel people to act in the name of any religion. In setting the appropriate boundaries of the Establishment Clause cases, the Court has frequently relied on our holding in *Lemon* for guidance, and we do so here. . . ."[63]

Although the term "free exercise" is not used (it is in Justice Sandra Day O'Connor's concurring opinion), it is quite obvious that it was what was intended (the plural "Religion *Clauses*" is used), supporting basic unanimity.

The unemployment compensation issue came to the Supreme Court again in the 1987 case of *Hobbie v. Unemployment Appeals Commission of Florida.*[64] The special feature of that case was that Paula Hobbie had converted to the Seventh-day Adventist Church after two and one-half years of employment, and quit when she was required to continue working on Saturdays. The Court, in an opinion by Justice Brennan (again over Justice Rehnquist's single dissent) ruled that the free exercise principles of *Sherbert* and *Thomas* were applicable even though Hobbie had been willing to work on Saturdays when she took the job.

As in *Sherbert* and *Thomas*, the defendant argued that awarding benefits to a Sabbatarian which would be denied to others violated the Establishment Clause. Again, the argument was dismissed. The Court, said Brennan, had "long recognized that the government may (and sometimes must) accommodate religious practices and that it may do so without violating the Establishment Clause. . . . As in *Sherbert*, the accommodation at issue here does not entangle the State in an unlawful fostering of religion."[65] As of this writing, the latest Supreme Court decision relating to a religion conflict between a government and a claimant to unemployment compensation benefits is *Frazee v. Illinois Department of Employment Security*.[66] Frazee was denied benefits because he refused as a Christian to accept a job that required him to work on Sundays because it was "the Lord's day." The trouble, however, was that he did not belong to any particular Christian sect, relying instead upon scripture, Exodus 20:8, 9, 10, which reads: "Remember the Sabbath day by keeping it holy. Six days you shall labour and do all your work but the seventh day is a Sabbath to the Lord your God. On it you shall not do any work."[67]

The Illinois court distinguished *Sherbert*, *Thomas*, and *Hobbie* in that the claimants in those cases were members of established religious sects or churches whereas Frazee was not: "What [the court rhetorically asked] would Sunday be today if professional football, baseball, basketball and tennis were barred. Today Sunday is not only a day for religion, but for recreation and labor. Today the supermarkets are open, service stations dispense fuel, utilities continue to serve the people and factories continue to belch smoke and tangible products [concluding that if] all Americans were to abstain from working on Sunday, chaos would result."[68]

The U.S. Supreme Court, in a unanimous opinion by Justice White which included even Chief Justice William H. Rehnquist, was not persuaded. They did not believe that there would be a mass movement away from Sunday employ if William Frazee succeeded in his claim. *Sherbert*, *Thomas*, and *Hobbie* were in point and had to be followed.

For present purposes the most noteworthy aspect of *Frazee* may be that the defendant did not even raise an Establishment Clause defense. Perhaps the uniform rejection of that argument in previous cases discouraged any further reliance on it. What is more generally significant is that the Court refused to analyze these employment cases as clashes between establishment and free exercise, although it could easily have done do. These opinions are thus clear examples of the Court's preference to avoid finding conflicts between the two branches of the religion clauses.

The Supreme Court in *Corporation of Presiding Bishop of the Church of Jesus Christ of Latter-day Saints* (Mormons) *v. Amos*,[69] rejected another purported clash between Establishment and Free Exercise in the employment area. The case involved Section 702 of the Civil Rights Act of 1964. In general the civil rights law prohibits discrimination on the basis of religion, but Section 702 excludes from its coverage (and thus allows) religious institutions to employ "individuals of a particular religion" to carry out their activities.

For some sixteen years plaintiff Mayson worked at the Church's gymnasium as a building engineer. He was fired in 1981 because he did not meet certain religious standards, e.g., regular church attendance, tithing and abstinence from coffee, tea, alcohol, and tobacco. Mayson and others brought suit against the Church alleging violation of the 1964 Act and asserting that, if Section 702 applied to shield the Church from liability, it was unconstitutional under the Establishment Clause.

The Church, by contrast, argued that Section 702 was not only constitutional, it was required by the Free Exercise Clause.

The District Court adjudged the Act unconstitutional for advancing religion in violation of the effect part of the purpose-effect-entanglement test. The District Court found that Mayson's job responsibilities were purely secular, and it rejected the Church's defense that the exemption was needed to avoid entanglement and to meet the requirements of the Free Exercise Clause. The Supreme Court, on direct appeal, reversed the District Court decision in an opinion by Justice White.

The District Court had determined that the legitimate purpose of the 1972 amendment was to minimize governmental interference with the decision-making process in religions, and with this Justice White agreed. The District Court, however, said that Section 702 unconstitutionally enabled religious organizations to advance their purposes at the expense of the religious beliefs of those of their employees who worked in nonreligious jobs, and with this Justice White did not agree. A law is not unconstitutional, he said, "simply because it *allows* churches to advance religion, which is their very purpose. For a law to have forbidden 'effects' under *Lemon*, it must be fair to say that the *government itself* has advanced religion through its own activities and influence."[70] The Court, he continued, had never indicated that statutes which gave special consideration to religious groups were necessarily invalid. "That would run contrary to the teaching of our cases that there is ample room for accommodation of religion under the Establishment Clause."[71]

Nor was he impressed with the argument that Congress could have limited its exemption to religious activities of churches, instead of including the work of secular employees like Mayson. The difficulty with that approach (which had in fact been the law until 1972) was that the line between secular and religious was not always clear, and churches could not be sure the courts would draw it the way the church would. "Fear of potential liability might affect the way an organization carried

out what it understood to be its religious mission."[72] The
broader exemption avoided this danger.

As for the free exercise rights of Mayson, White acknowl-
edged that his liberty was impinged upon, "but it was the
Church . . . and not the Government, who put him to the choice
of changing his religious practices or losing his job."[73]
Ultimately, what seemed to persuade the Court was that
Mayson was no worse off than he would have been if the 1964
Act had never been passed. Having found no Establishment
Clause violation, the Court had "no occasion to pass on the argu-
ment . . . that the exemption . . . is required by the Free Exercise
Clause.[74]

Justice Brennan, concurring, also found no conflict between
the Establishment and Free Exercise Clauses in the case. Indeed,
in his view the case involved a "confrontation between the [free
exercise] rights of religious organizations and those of
individuals."[75] On the one hand, Mayson should not be forced
to change either his religion or his job. On the other hand,
"religious organizations have an interest in autonomy in order-
ing their internal affairs."[76] It would hardly do, for instance, to
forbid a church to dismiss a minister who had converted to
another religion.

Ideally, Justice Brennan said, religious organizations should
be able to discriminate only with respect to religious activities.
However, in respect to nonprofit religious organizations there is
a danger that they may be deterred from classifying as religious
those activities which they regard as religious but others may
not. This substantial potential for chilling religious activity
justifies a categorical exemption for nonprofit activities. Insofar
as Section 702 applied to *for-profit* activities of churches, though,
Brennan would deem it unconstitutional.

Only Justice Sandra Day O'Connor, also concurring in the
result, felt called upon to deal with the relationship between the
Establishment and Free Exercise Clauses. She reiterated her

view, expressed in *Wallace v. Jaffree*,[77] that an exemption statute like Section 702 "*does* have the effect of advancing religion. The necessary second step is to separate those benefits to religion that constitutionally accommodate the free exercise of religion from those that provide unjustifiable awards of assistance to religious organizations."[78] Section 702, she concluded, was a constitutionally permissible accommodation, at least as applied to not-for-profit activities. Justice O'Connor, however, was alone in this aspect of her analysis.

Another example of the Supreme Court's refusing to face a conflict between the Establishment and Free Exercise Clauses was *Widmar v. Vincent*.[79] The University of Missouri at Kansas City had a policy of allowing student groups the use of its facilities. An Evangelical Christian student group applied for permission to use University facilities for its meetings. The University refused, based on its policy that, as a state institution, it did not allow organized religious activities except at chapels. The students challenged the constitutionality of the University's policy, and the case reached the Supreme Court.

If ever a case seemed to present a conflict between Establishment and Free Exercise, this one did. On one side, the students, organized under the name Cornerstone, claimed a free exercise and also equal protection and free speech rights to use the University's facilities. The University, on the other side, claimed it was forbidden by the Establishment Clause to make such facilities available.

In an opinion by Justice Lewis F. Powell, with only Justice White dissenting, the Court held that the University's policy violated, neither the Free Exercise nor the Establishment Clause, but the Free Speech Clause. Analyzing the student group's religious meetings as a form of speech, the Court determined that treating them differently from other groups was discrimination against one set of ideas as opposed to others. The University, said Justice Powell, "misconceives the nature of this case." "The question is not whether the creation of a religious forum would violate the Establishment Clause. The University has opened its facilities for use by student groups, and the question is whether it can now exclude groups because of the content of their speech."[80]

So framed, the answer to the question was obviously "No." The Court, therefore, did not need to "inquire into the extent, if any, to which free exercise interests are infringed by the challenged University regulation." Nor did it "reach the questions that would arise if state accommodation of Free Exercise and Free Speech rights should, in a particular case, conflict with the prohibitions of the Establishment Clause."[81]

Texas Monthly, Inc. v. Bullock[82] is, at this writing the most recent decision (or perhaps decisions) relating to the subject of this essay. It deals with a statute that exempted from sales and use taxes periodicals published or distributed by a religious faith consisting wholly of writings promulgating the teaching of the faith and books consisting wholly of writings sacred to it. Suit challenging the constitutionality of the statute was brought by *Texas Monthly*, a magazine that did not qualify for the exemption. The outcome was a judgment upholding the plaintiff's claim of unconstitutionality but not with a single opinion.

To Justice Brennan (speaking also for Justices Marshall and John Paul Stevens) the statute was not unconstitutional simply because it benefited religion, but because it benefited *only* religion.

Insofar as [a governmental] subsidy is conferred upon a wide array of nonsectarian groups as well as religious organizations in pursuit of some legitimate secular end, the fact that religious groups benefit incidentally does not deprive the subsidy of the secular purpose and primary effect mandated by the Establishment Clause. However, when government directs a subsidy exclusively to religious organizations that is not required by the Free Exercise Clause and that either burdens nonbeneficiaries markedly or cannot reasonably be seen as removing a

significant state-imposed deterrent to the free exercise of religion, as
Texas has done . . . it "provides unjustifiable awards of assistance to
religious organizations" and cannot but convey a "message of
endorsement" to slighted members of the community. This is particularly true where, as here, the subsidy is targeted at writings that
promulgate the teachings of religious faiths. It is difficult to view Texas'
narrow exemption as anything but state sponsorship of religious belief,
regardless whether one adopts the perspective of beneficiaries or of
uncompensated contributors.[83]

The State of Texas argued that it was required by the Free
Exercise Clause to grant a tax exemption to religious
publications. Despite some dictum from two Supreme Court
decisions of the 1940s,[84] Justice Brennan rejected the claim.
Citing the *Bob Jones University* case discussed previously, he
explained that the law was not clear that tax exemption for
religious activities are not constitutionally mandated. On the
contrary, such exemptions are inconsistent with the Establishment Clause if they impose substantial burdens on
nonbeneficiaries and do not remove governmentally-imposed
burdens on religious practices. "Neither the Free Exercise Clause
nor the Establishment Clause prevents Texas from withdrawing
its current exemption for religious publications if it chooses not
to expand it to promote some legitimate secular aim" [i.e., all or
nothing].[85]

Justice White found the exemption to be unconstitutional
under the Free Press Clause; his opinion therefore need not be
considered here.

To Justice Harry Blackmun (joined by Justice O'Connor)
Brennan's opinion subordinated the Free Exercise Clause to the
Establishment Clause, while upholding the exemption would
subordinate the Establishment to the Free Exercise Clause. In his
view, there was no need to choose between them. The Court did
not have to decide the extent to which the Free Exercise Clause
requires a tax exemption for the sale of religious literature by

religious organizations. He therefore refused to join Justice Brennan in rejecting the earlier precedents. It was sufficient to determine whether a tax exemption *limited* to the sale of religious literature by religious organizations violates the Establishment Clause. To him it did. "A statutory preference for the dissemination of religious ideas offends our most basic understanding of what the Establishment Clause is all about and hence is constitutionally intolerable."[86]

This author finds something amusing in the opening paragraph of Justice Antonin Scalia's dissenting opinion (with which Chief Justice Rehnquist and Justice Anthony M. Kennedy concurred.) Here is how it reads, with this writer's comments:

As a judicial demolition project, today's decision is impressive. The machinery employed by the opinions of Justice Brennan and Justice Blackmun is no more substantial than the antinomy that accommodation of religion may be required but not permitted, and the bold but unsupportable assertion (given such realities as the text of the Declaration of Independence [written before there was an Article VI or First Amendment to the Constitution], the national Thanksgiving Day proclamated by every President since Lincoln [and objected to as unconstitutional by Presidents Jefferson, Madison, and Jackson wherefore Scalia started with Lincoln], the inscription on our coins [imposed upon law-abiding American citizens like McCollom, Torcaso, and Jaffree who do not trust in God because to them there is no God], the words of our Pledge of Allegiance [which did not have the words "under God" in it from the time it was created in 1892 until they were put in it by Congressional statute in 1954], the invocation with which sessions of our Court are opened and, come to think of it, the discriminatory protection of freedom of religion in the Constitution) that government may not "convey a message of endorsement of religion."[87]

The crux of Justice Scalia's dissent was that Justice Brennan's opinion (and presumably also Justice Blackmun's) was inconsistent with American traditions, and, perhaps to a lesser extent, with prior Court opinions. He said, "It is not right—it is not constitutionally healthy—that this Court should feel authorized to refashion anew our civil society's relationship with religion, adopting a theory of church and state that is contradicted by current practice, tradition, and even our own case law."[88]

According to Justice Scalia, religious tax exemptions permeate state and federal codes, and have done so for many years. The constitutional principle of state accommodation to religion goes as far back as the *Zorach* opinion in 1952. Justice Scalia admitted that the aspects of the earlier opinions emphasized by Justice Brennan could be found in them, but he insisted that they were not crucial to the holdings. The point is debatable. But, this essay suggests, assuming Justice Scalia was correct, this would not be the first time, nor will it be the last, that desirable new law is made by reading it into well-established old law.

For present purposes, the important part of Justice Scalia's opinion is his view that the case presented no conflict between the Free Exercise and Establishment Clauses. The exemption was proper under the accommodation principle, he said, even if it was not required by the Free Exercise Clause. "If the exemption comes so close to being a constitutionally required accommodation, there is no doubt that it is at least a permissible one."[89]

In the case, *Jimmy Swaggart Ministries v. Board of Equalization of California*[90] the Court held that California's imposition of sales and use tax liability on appellant's sales of religious materials does not contravene the religion clauses of the First Amendment. Argued before the Supreme Court 31 October 1989, *Jimmy Swaggart* raised a host of constitutional questions dealing with taxability of mail order and across-the-table sales by a not-for-profit evangelical institution of religious books, records, and tapes as well as other religious merchandise. Unlike Texas, California's law does not provide an exemption from its sales tax for religious goods. The Swaggart ministries' claims that the failure to provide such an exemption itself violates the Free

Exercise Clause, as well as the Establishment Clause, the Commerce Clause, the Due Process Clause, and the Ninth and Tenth Amendments. In terms of the organization of this essay, the case belongs in the category of plaintiffs' pleading both Establishment and Free Exercise claims.

CONCLUSION

To those judges, scholars, and lawyers committed to a strict separation of church and state—often called absolutists or extremists or doctrinaire or unrealistic or uncompromising (in contrast to "accommodationists" or "non-preferentialists") —decisions such as *Texas Monthly* bring considerable satisfaction for they avoid rulings in which the Establishment and Free Exercise Clauses can be played against one another. From a purely scholarly point of view, the decision is of interest because it indicates that the unity of the two clauses is accepted both by separationists and accommodationists on the Court. Justice Scalia no more than Justice Brennan believes that the two clauses are in conflict. Indeed, it is noteworthy that, for example, Justices Brennan and Marshall, the separationists, and Justices Rehnquist and Scalia, the non-preferentialists, divide not only on the Establishment Clause cases such as *Texas Monthly*, but on Free Exercise Clause cases as well, with Justice Brennan favoring stricter protection for religious practices and Rehnquist being more accommodating to governmental policies. Thus, in *Lyng v. Northwest Indian Cemetery Protective Association*,[91] Justices Rehnquist and Scalia joined in an opinion upholding against a free exercise challenge of a Forest Service project to develop a portion of a national forest used by Indians for religious purposes, while Justices Brennan and Marshall dissented. The latter two similarly dissented from Justice Rehnquist's opinion (Scalia was not yet on the Court) rejecting the Free Exercise claims of a Jewish officer in the U.S. Air Force against a regulation forbidding him to wear a hat (yarmulke) as his religion demanded.[92] It is because both sides accept the unity of the religion clauses that these consistent patterns occur.

A merger of Establishment and Free Exercise is hardly new. It goes back to Roger Williams, Thomas Paine, Thomas Jefferson, and James Madison among many others. Within the past decade that merger has been challenged and rejected by many as never having existed or not now existing, especially by those unhappy to a greater or lesser extent with the Establishment Clause altogether, since conflicts between Establishment and Free Exercise must, they believe, obviously be decided in favor of the latter.

The author of this article is a strict church-state separationist, and also (consequently) a strict supporter of religious liberty. From this perspective, Establishment-Free Exercise unity seems plausible and even natural (especially since as a practicing attorney he defends both positions). Be that as it may, on the whole the Supreme Court cases considered here support an Establishment-Free Exercise unity. Whether this will continue as the U.S. Supreme Court now stands and will stand for a number of years, is far from certain.

NOTES

1. Leo Pfeffer, "Freedom and/or Separation: The Constitutional Dilemma of the First Amendment," *Minnesota Law Review* 64 (1980):561.
2. "Congress shall make no law respecting an establishment of religion or prohibiting the free exercise thereof. . . ."
3. Leo Pfeffer, "The Case for Separation" in *Religion in America*, ed. John Cogley (New York: Meridian Books, 1958), 52-60.
4. Philip B. Kurland, "Of Church and State and the Supreme Court," *University of Chicago Law Review* 29 (Autumn 1961):1-96.
5. Philip Kurland, *Religion and the Law: Of Church and State and the Supreme Court* (Chicago: Aldine Publishing Co., 1962).
6. Ibid., 112.

7. Bette Novit Evans, "Contradictory Demands on the First Amendment Religion Clauses: Having It Both Ways," *Journal of Church and State* 30 (Autumn 1988):465.

8. *Everson v. Board of Education*, 330 U.S. 1 (1947) at 40. Although Justice Rutledge's statement was made in a dissenting opinion, there was no disagreement with this point in the majority opinion.

9. Roger Williams, *The Bloudy Tenet of Persecution for Cause of Conscience* (1644); quoted in Leo Pfeffer, *Church, State and Freedom*, rev. ed. (Boston: Beacon Press, 1967), 87.

10. James Madison, "Memorial and Remonstrance Against Religious Assessments" (1785); reprinted in appendix in *Everson* at 64.

11. Virginia Statute of Religious Liberty; reprinted in Phillip Kurland and Ralph Lerner, eds., *The Founders' Constitution*, 5 vols. (Chicago: University of Chicago Press, 1987), 5:84.

12. Reprinted in ibid., 5:69.

13. Quoted by Justice Rutledge in *Everson* at 39n. 27.

14. Reprinted in Kurland and Lerner, *Founder's Constitution*, 5:98.

15. *Reynolds v. United States*, 98 U.S. 145 (1878) at 164.

16. James Bryce, *The American Commonwealth*, 3rd ed. (New York: Macmillan Company, 1910), 2:766.

17. Jeremiah S. Black, "Essay on Religious Liberty," in *Essays and Speeches of Jeremiah S. Black*, ed. Chauncey F. Black (New York: D. Appleton and Company, 1886), 53. Quoted by Justice Brennan, concurring in *Abington School District v. Schempp* 374 U.S. 203, 230 (1963) at 304 (emphasis by Brennan).

18. *Everson* at 32.

19. Ibid. at 15-16. This language parallels the interpretation of the First Amendment provided by Charles Beard a few years earlier: "Congress can make no law respecting an establishment of religion. This means that Congress cannot adopt any form of religion as the national religion. It cannot set up one church as the national church, establish its creed, lay taxes generally to support it, compel people to attend it, and punish them for nonattendance. Nor can Congress any more vote money for the support of all churches than it can establish one of them as a national church. That would be a form of establishment." *The Republic* (New York: Viking Press, 1944), 165.

20. *Zorach v. Clauson*, 343 U.S. 306 (1952).

21. Ibid. at 308.

22. Pfeffer, *Church, State and Freedom*, 415.
23. *Zorach* at 311.
24. Ibid. at 312.
25. Leah Cunn, a former pupil in a Brooklyn public school, swore in an affidavit as follows:

"When the released time students departed at 2:00 P.M. on Wednesdays, I felt left behind. The released children made remarks about my being Jewish and I was made very much aware of the fact that I did not participate with them in the released time program. I endured a great deal of anguish as a result of this and decided that I would like to go along with the other children to the church center rather than continue to expose myself to such harassment. I asked my mother for permission to participate in the released time program and to accompany my Catholic classmates to their religious center, but she forbade it." Quoted from Pfeffer, *Church, State and Freedom*, 417.

Esta Gluck [mother of a public school pupil] swore that:

"Miss Jeffries, a second and third grade teacher at P.S. 130 in Brooklyn, was very active in soliciting student participation in released time for religious instruction. Such activities were carried on by Miss Jeffries both on and off the school premises and both during and after school hours. She visited parents for the purpose of recruiting Catholic students for released time and her activities in this respect is common neighborhood knowledge."

"During the Spring 1950 semester I called to the attention of Mr. Lubell (the principal) another incident in which Miss Jeffries had participated. A student in her class became ill and vomited in the classroom. Miss Jeffries said to the sick student that she did not object to looking at the vomit as much as she objected to looking at the student's face because he did not participate in the released time program. Mr. Lubell was shocked and told me that he would speak to Miss Jeffries about the incident." Ibid., 421-22.

(It should be noted that remarks like these in substance if not in quite the same wording are more likely to be found in the post-

Vatican II era among evangelical Protestants than those of the
Roman Catholic faith.

26.   *Zorach* at 315.

27.   There is considerable and ever-growing literature on this subject,
      e.g., Arlin M. Adams and Sarah Barringer Gordon, "The Doctrine
      of Accommodation in the Jurisprudence of the Religion Clauses,"
      De Paul Law Review 37 (Spring 1988) 317-45. The authors define it
      as follows:

      In *Zorach v. Clauson*, written by Justice Douglas in 1952, the
      Supreme Court upheld a released-time program that permitted
      public school children to be dismissed from class in order to
      receive religious instruction at parochial schools and churches.
      The Court reasoned that the arrangement did not violate the
      Establishment Clause, because it accommodated rather than
      advanced religious interests. Actions that fall within the zone of
      permissible accommodation adjust governmental regulations to
      the religious needs of citizens, Justice Douglas reasoned, without
      transgressing the prohibitions of the Establishment Clause.

      "'Permissible accommodation' may thus be defined as an area of
      allowable governmental deference to the religious requirements of
      a pluralistic society in which a variety of religious beliefs are
      deeply held." Ibid., 319 (footnotes omitted).

28.   Justice Robert H. Jackson, in dissent, objected to this attribution.
      "As one whose children, as a matter of free choice, have been sent
      to privately supported Church schools," he said, "I may challenge
      the Court's suggestion that opposition to this plan can only be
      antireligious, atheistic, or agnostic." *Zorach* at 324.

29.   *Lemon v. Kurtzman*, 403 U.S. 602 (1971) at 612-13 (citations
      omitted).

30.   The exception is the legislative prayer case, *Marsh v. Chambers*, 463
      U.S. 783 (1983).

31.   The *Everson* and *Lemon* formulas are both quoted most recently in
      *County of Allegheny v. American Civil Liberties Union Greater
      Pittsburgh Chapter*, 109 S. Ct. 3086 (1989) at 3090, 3100.

32.   Wilber G. Katz, "Freedom of Religion and State Neutrality,"
      University of Chicago Law Review 20 (1953): 426.

33.   Laurence Tribe, *American Constitutional Law*, 1st ed. (Mineola, N.Y.:

Foundation Press, 1978), 814-15, 833; 2nd ed., 1988, 1156-57, 1201. NP. 8, fn 33.

34. Pfeffer, "Freedom and/or Separation," 583-84.

35. *Larson v. Valente*, 456 U.S. 228 (1982).

36. Ibid. at 245.

37. *Hernandez v. Commissioner of Internal Revenue*, 109 S. Ct. 2136 (1989).

38. Ibid. at 2141.

39. *United States v. Lee*, 455 U.S. 252 (1982).

40. *Bob Jones University v. United States*, 461 U.S. 574 (1983).

41. Ibid. at 604 n. 30.

42. *Harris v. McRae*, 448 U.S. 297 (1980).

43. Ibid. at 319. It should be noted that, although the Court referred only to Protestant and Jewish briefs, an amicus curiae brief endorsing this argument was submitted by, among others, an organization called Catholics for a Free Choice.

44. *Tony and Susan Alamo Foundation v. Secretary of Labor*, 471 U.S. 294 (1985).

45. Ibid. at 303.

46. Ibid. at 305-06.

47. *Wisconsin v. Yoder*, 406 U.S. 205 (1972).

48. Ibid. at 215.

49. Ibid. at 221.

50. *Walz v. Tax Commission*, 397 U.S. (1970) at 664, 672, quoted in *Yoder* at 221.

51. *Yoder* at 234 n. 22.

52. *Heisler v. Board of Review*, 343 U.S. 939 (1952).

53. The issue had reached the Court in *Kut v. Bureau of Unemployment Compensation of Ohio*, 329 U.S. 669 (1946), but there the appeal was dismissed because there was an independent reason under state law to justify the result.

54. *Sherbert v. Verner*, 374 U.S. 398 (1963).

55. Ibid. at 404.

56. Ibid. at 409.

57. Ibid. at 415 (Emphasis in original).

58. *In re Jenison*, 375 U.S. 14 (1963).

59. *In re Jenison* 125 N.W. 2d 588 (1964).

60. *Thomas v. Review Board of Indiana*, 450 U.S. 707 (1981).

61. Ibid. at 719.

62. *Estate of Thornton v. Caldor, Inc.,* 472 U.S. 703 (1985).

63. Ibid. at 708.

64. *Hobbie v. Unemployment Appeals Commission of Florida,* 480 U.S. 136 (1987).

65. Ibid. at 1051.

66. *Frazee v. Illinois Department of Employment Security,* 109 S. Ct. 1514 (1989).

67. Ibid. at 1517 n. 1.

68. Quoted in ibid. at 1518.

69. *Corporation of Presiding Bishop of the Church of Jesus Christ of Latter-day Saints (Mormons) v. Amos,* 483 U.S. 327 (1987).

70. Ibid. at 2868-69 (emphasis in original).

71. Ibid. at 2869.

72. Ibid. at 2868.

73. Ibid. at 2869 n. 15.

74. Ibid. at 2870 n. 17.

75. Ibid. at 2870.

76. Ibid. at 2871.

77. *Wallace v. Jaffree,* 472 U.S. 38 (1985) at 67.

78. *Amos* at 2874.

79. *Widmar v. Vincent,* 454 U.S. 263 (1981).

80. Ibid. at 273.

81. Ibid. at 275 n. 13.

82. *Texas Monthly, Inc. v. Bullock,* 109 S. Ct. 890 (1989).

83. Ibid. at 899-900 (emphasis in original; citations and footnotes omitted).

84. *Murdock v. Commonwealth of Pennsylvania,* 319 U.S. 105 (1943); *Follett v. Town of McCormick,* 321 U.S. 573 (1944).

85. *Texas Monthly, Inc.* at 903.

86. Ibid. at 907.

87. Ibid.

88. Ibid. at 916.

89. Ibid. at 914.

90. *Jimmy Swaggart Ministries v. Board of Education of California,* 109 S.Ct. 688 (1990).

91. *Lyng v. Northwest Indian Cemetery Protective Association,* 485 U. S. 139 (1988).

92. *Goldman v. Weinberger,* 475 U.S. 503 (1986).

A SELECTED BIBLIOGRAPHY

Abraham, Henry J. *Freedom and the Court: Civil Rights and Liberties in the United States.* 4th ed. New York: Oxford University Press, 1982.

Alley, Robert S., ed. *James Madison on Religious Liberty.* Buffalo, N.Y.: Prometheus Books, 1985.

Berns, Walter. *The First Amendment and the Future of American Democracy.* New York: Basic Books, Inc., 1976.

Bonomi, Patricia U. *Under the Cope of Heaven: Religion, Society, and Politics in Colonial America.* New York: Oxford University Press, 1986.

Brant, Irving. *The Bill of Rights: Its Origin and Meaning.* Indianapolis: The Bobb-Merrill Co., Inc., 1965.

Clebsch, William A. *From Sacred to Profane America: The Role of Religion in American History.* New York: Harper and Row, 1968.

Cobb, Sanford H. *The Rise of Religious Liberty in America: A History.* New York: The Macmillan Co., 1902.

Conley, Patrick T. and Kaminski, John P., eds. *The Constitution and the States: The Role of the Original Thirteen in the Framing and Adoption of the Federal Constitution.* Madison, Wis.: Madison House, sponsored by the U. S. Constitution Council of the Thirteen Original States and the Center for the Study of the American Constitution, 1988.

This Constitution: From Ratification to the Bill of Rights. Washington, D.C.: Congressional Quarterly Books, 1988. A joint publication of the American Political Science

Association, the American Historical Association, and Congressional Quarterly, Inc.

Cousins, Norman, ed. *'In God We Trust': The Religious Beliefs and Ideas of American Founding Fathers*. New York: Harper and Brothers, 1958.

Curry, Thomas J. *The First Freedoms: Church and State in America to the Passage of the First Amendment*. New York: Oxford University Press, 1986.

DePauw, Linda Grant, ed. *Documentary History of the First Federal Congress of the United States of America*. 9 vols. Baltimore: Johns Hopkins University Press, 1972.

Elliot, Jonathan, ed. *The Debates in the Several State Conventions on the Adoption of the Federal Constitution*. 2d ed. Philadelphia: J. B. Lippincott, 1896.

Estep, William R. *Revolution Within the Revolution: The First Amendment in Historical Context, 1612-1789*. Grand Rapids, Mich.: Wm. B. Eerdmans Publishing Co., 1990.

Gaustad, Edwin Scott. *Faith of Our Fathers: Religion and the New Nation*. San Francisco: Harper and Row, 1987.

Gillespie, Michael Allen and Michael Lienesch, eds. *Ratifying the Constitution*. Lawrence: University Press of Kansas, 1989.

Howe, Mark De Wolf. *The Garden and the Wilderness: Religion and Government in Constitutional History*. Chicago: University of Chicago Press, 1965.

Hudson, Winthrop S. *The Great Tradition of the American Churches.* New York: Harper and Row, 1953.

Humphrey, Edward F. *Nationalism and Religion in America, 1774-1789.* New York: Russell and Russell, 1965. Reprint of 1924 edition.

Hunt, George L., ed. *Calvinism and the Political Order.* Philadelphia: The Westminster Press, 1965.

Jensen, Merrill, ed. *Ratification of the Constitution of the United States.* 7 vols. Madison: State Historical Society of Wisconsin, 1976.

Kauper, Paul G. *Religion and the Constitution.* Baton Rouge: Louisiana State University Press, 1964.

Kurland, Philip B. and Robert Lerners, eds. *The Founders' Constitution.* 5 vols. Chicago: University of Chicago Press, 1957.

Kurland, Philip B., ed. *Church and State: The Supreme Court and the First Amendment.* Chicago: University of Chicago Press, 1975.

Levinson, Sanford. *Constitutional Faith.* Princeton: Princeton Univesity Press, 1988.

Levy, Leonard W., ed. *Encyclopedia of the American Constitution.* 4 vols. New York: The Macmillan Co., 1986.

_____, ed. *Essays on the Making of the Constitution.* 2nd ed. New York: Oxford University Press, 1987.

_____. *The Establishment Clause: Religion and the First Amendment.* New York: The Macmillan Publishing Co., 1986.

_____ and Dennis J. Mahoney. *The Framing and Ratification of the Constitution.* New York: The Macmillan Publishing Co., 1987.

_____. *Original Intent and the Framers' Constitution.* New York: The Macmillan Co., 1988.

Marnell, William H. *The First Amendment: The History of Religious Freedom in America.* Garden City, N.Y.: Doubleday and Co., Inc., 1964.

Miller, William Lee. *The First Liberty: Religion and the American Republic.* New York: Alfred A. Knopf, 1986.

Morgan, Edmund S. *Roger Williams: The Church and the State.* New York: Harcourt, Brace, and World, 1967.

Peterson, Merrill D. and Robert C. Vaughan, eds. *The Virginia Statute for Religious Freedom: Its Evolution and Consequences in American History.* New York: Cambridge University Press, 1988.

Pfeffer, Leo. *Church, State, and Freedom.* Rev. ed. Boston: Beacon Press, 1967.

_____. *God, Caesar, and the Constitution: The Court as Referee in Church-State Confrontation.* Boston: Beacon Press, 1975.

Richards, David A. J. *Toleration and the Constitution.* New York: Oxford University Press, 1986.

Rutland, Robert Allen. *The Birth of the Bill of Rights.* Rev. ed. Boston: Northeastern University Press, 1983.

_____. *James Madison: The Founding Father.* New York: The Macmillan Publishing Co., 1987.

Semonche, John E. *Religion and Constitutional Government in the United States: A Historical Overview with Sources.* Carrboro, N.C.: Signal Books, 1985.

Sorauf, Frank. *The Wall of Separation: The Constitutional Politics of Church and State.* Princeton: Princeton University Press, 1976.

Smith, Page. *The Constitution: A Documentary and Narrative History.* New York: William Morrow & Company, Inc., 1978.

Stokes, Anson Phelps. *Church and State in the United States.* 3 vols. New York: Harper and Brothers, 1950.

White, Ronald C., Jr., and Albright G. Zimmerman, eds. *Unsettled Arena: Religion and the Bill of Rights.* Grand Rapids: Wm. B. Eerdmans Publishing Co., 1989

Wilson, John F., ed. *Church and State in America: The Colonial and Early National Periods: A Bibliographical Guide.* New York: Greenwood Press, 1986.

Wood, James E., Jr., ed. *Religion and the State: Essays in Honor of Leo Pfeffer.* Waco, Texas: Baylor University Press, 1985.

INDEX